PARANORMAL
GLOUCESTERSHIRE

S. C. SKILLMAN

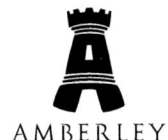

AMBERLEY

First published 2025

Amberley Publishing
The Hill, Stroud
Gloucestershire, GL5 4EP

www.amberley-books.com

British Library Cataloguing in Publication Data.
A catalogue record for this book is available from the British Library.

ISBN 978 1 3981 2280 2 (print)
ISBN 978 1 3981 2281 9 (ebook)

Typesetting by Hurix Digital, India.
Printed in Great Britain.

Appointed GPSR EU Representative: Easy Access System Europe Oü, 16879218
Address: Mustamäe tee 50, 10621, Tallinn, Estonia
Contact Details: gpsr.requests@easproject.com, +358 40 500 3575

Contents

Introduction

I am a stranger here in Gloucestershire:
These high wild hills and rough uneven ways
Draw out our miles.

Richard II, Act II, Scene 3

So says Henry Percy, Earl of Northumberland, in reply to Henry Bolingbroke, Duke of Hereford, according to William Shakespeare, when their journey on horseback to Berkeley Castle proves tough. Nowadays it's much easier to reach that particular stronghold, along with many other evocative and bewitching locations in Gloucestershire, all of them rich with multiple layers of uncanny tales. In researching this book, I found myself drawn in by the call of past human players upon the stage, from the mournful ambiance of a Neolithic long barrow to the now-serene nave of a great abbey which saw violent deeds hundreds of years ago. On the way I researched ancient houses where the imprint of highly charged past events remains locked into their very fabric.

Gloucestershire offers so many unworldly experiences that I sadly had to leave out several locations I visited and photographed. Perhaps they might form the basis of another book! I chose to include here those atmospheric places and stories which had the greatest impact on me. Numerous ghosts and spirits linger in Gloucestershire, re-enacting fateful stories that cannot fail to draw the curious with their emotional intensity, their mystery, or their poignancy.

1

Gloucester

Bring me into your city,
And I will use the olive with my sword,
Make war breed peace, make peace stint war, make each
Prescribe to other as each other's leech.

Timon of Athens, Act 5, Scene 4

Nearly 2,000 years of history have enriched the city of Gloucester with a multitude of ghostly tales. The town first emerged during the Roman occupation and gained status in AD 97 under Emperor Nerva. Gloucester also held out against a siege by Royalist forces in 1643, during the First English Civil War. We will hear more of that in the chapter on Chavenage, where I relate the macabre legend of supernatural vengeance upon the Parliamentary colonel who saved Gloucester on that occasion. The significance of this city during medieval times is emphasised by the high number of monastic establishments, of which St Peter's Abbey, founded in 679, later became the cathedral. What follows represents just a small selection of the unearthly events in the city today.

St Mary's Square

Determined Protestant convert Bishop John Hooper found favour in the reign of the fervently reformist boy-king Edward VI, and he was appointed Chaplain to the

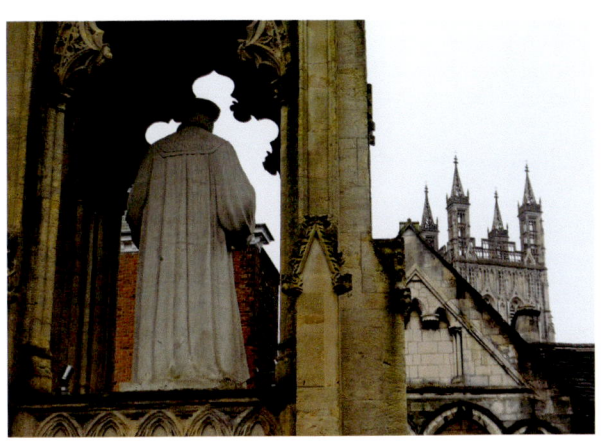

Bishop Hooper's Monument,
opposite Gloucester Cathedral.
(Courtesy of Jamie Robinson)

Protector, the Duke of Somerset. But his luck turned when Edward died aged fifteen and Catholic Mary I came to the throne. She sent him to the Fleet Prison in London for seventeen months. He refused her demands to recant, so he was returned to Gloucester and put to death in St Mary's Square. There were 7,000 spectators who gathered to witness his execution just outside St Mary's Gate. His spectre has since been sighted several times; he appears near the monument which marks the site of his burning at the stake in 1555, facing his own cathedral. Mary, who reigned from 1553 until her death in 1558, is also said to have haunted the area.

Gloucester Cathedral

Gloucester gained city status in 1541 following the Dissolution of the Monasteries and the transformation of the abbey into a cathedral. Many visitors have reported 'eerie echoes' here along with visions of monks drifting through the nave or the cloister. The building would have been frequented by monks from the time it came under the control of the Benedictine order at the beginning of the eleventh century.

Gloucester's magnificent cathedral stands at the centre of many fateful turning points in the story of Britain, including the downfall of Bishop Hooper. William the Conqueror held his Christmas court in the chapter house in 1085, and then made

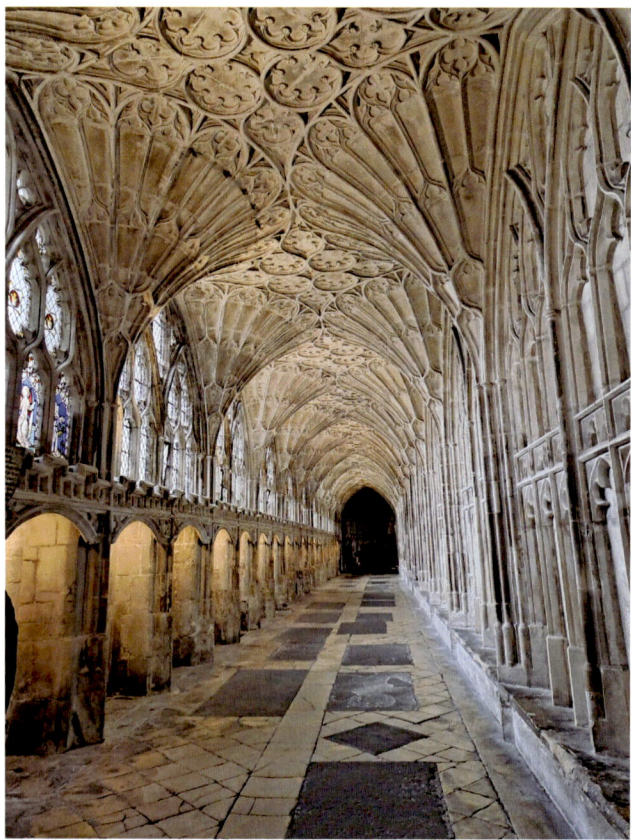

Cathedral cloister, Gloucester Cathedral.

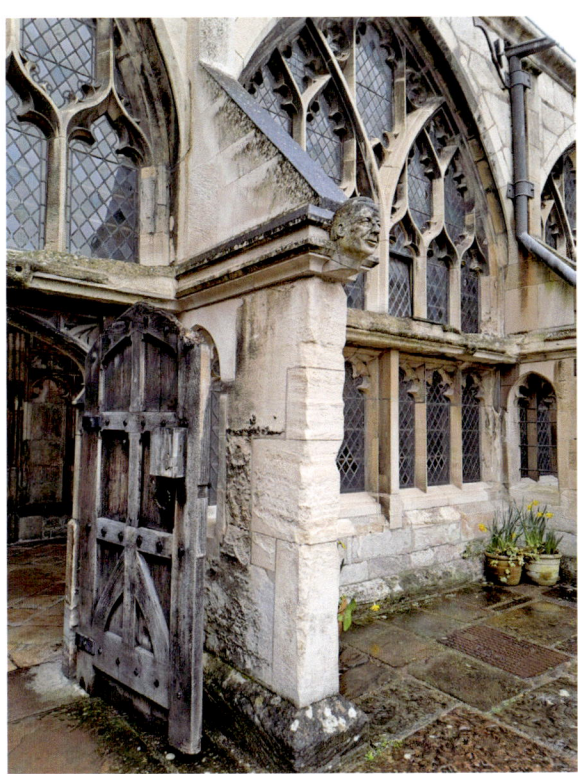

Door into the cloister, Gloucester Cathedral.

a momentous decision. As author John O'Farrell puts it in his book *An Utterly Impartial History of Britain*:

> By Christmas 1085, with his kingdom finally secure, the now rather corpulent King William held court at Gloucester, revelling and drinking and debating what the regime should do next. It was clearly a fun Christmas because they emerged from the festivities with one exciting, madcap idea; they were going to carry out a really thorough tax assessment.

This, of course, was the Domesday Book. Just over 130 years later, in 1216, the chapter house again served as an important venue when it hosted the coronation of Henry III, aged nine years, with a gilded iron ring. Edward II – whose remains may or may not be interred in the lavishly carved shrine erected by his son in 1327 – is also commemorated here. His state funeral and the highly ornamented shrine with its many-pinnacled canopy gave the abbey a new source of revenue to draw the pilgrims in.

Nowadays, a plaque by the tomb acknowledges, 'Edward's poor judgement lost him the confidence of the people and his throne'. At the time he was said to have died from an illness at Berkeley Castle, but many discrepancies challenge that claim. Lord Berkeley initially reported his death, and a few years later was denying he even knew about it. A grisly story arose in 1330 about how Edward had actually been despatched. For alternative theories by historians as to whether this shrine really does contain the remains of Edward II, read my chapter on the much-haunted Berkeley Castle.

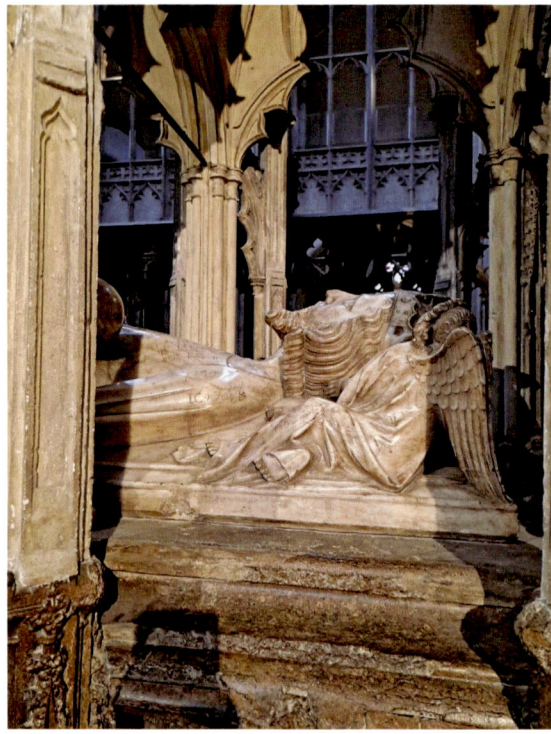

Edward II's tomb, Gloucester
Cathedral.

Then, 200 years after the Dissolution of the Monasteries, the cathedral underwent much restoration. It is from this period that another ghost story may have originated. A number of visitors have claimed sightings of a spectral form believed to be that of a fourteen-year-old boy who fell to his death from the scaffolding during the restoration work in the eighteenth and nineteenth centuries.

The cathedral has frequently been used as a filming location and served as a stand-in for Hogwarts in the Harry Potter films; fans will recognise the cloisters as the location of the appearance of the mysterious message 'The Chamber of Secrets has been opened' and the undignified treatment of Argus Filch's cat.

Gloucester Prison

The old Gloucester Prison has earned a reputation for eerie ghost stories; visitors and staff alike have often reported unsettling encounters. Most striking of these may be the regular appearances of a phantom named Jenny. The prison opened in 1791, incarcerating serious offenders until its closure in 2013. During that time Jenny often made her presence known; she was murdered on the site in the fifteenth century – long before the prison was constructed. During the prison's years in use Jenny appeared to both inmates and guards seeming to indicate the spot where she lost her life. In 1969 some prisoners in cell 25 on the A4 landing held a séance, hoping to communicate with her, and ended up fleeing to avoid the books and flowerpots thrown around the room by an unseen force.

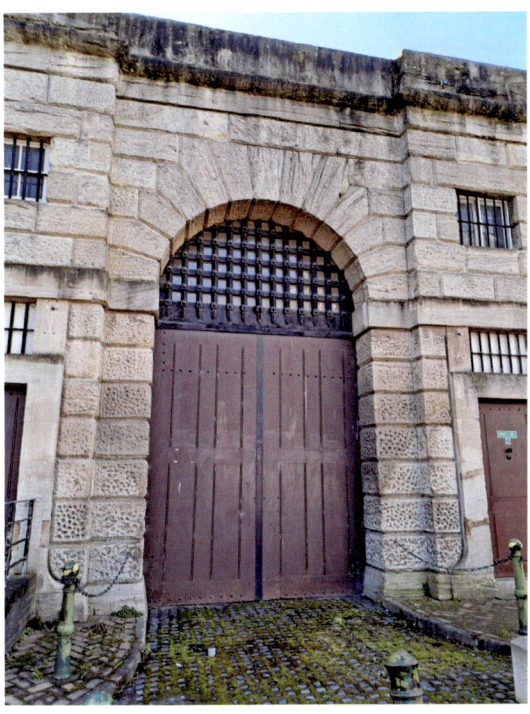

Main doors of the old prison, Gloucester.

When alive, Jenny was held in the cells of the nearby abbey and those who reported seeing her claimed she had mocked and taunted them; they thought she'd been searching for her murderer, returning to the prison every night in her quest for revenge, with unearthly activity particularly strong in cell 25.

Another frequent visitation is said to be that of Amelia Dyer, notorious Victorian baby farmer. The prison's most infamous execution took place in 1879 when Amelia was sentenced to death. Her execution drew immense public attention. Sightings of her, often accompanied by the sound of a woman's sobs, have been reported in and around the execution chamber. One particularly chilling tale tells of a visitor who, while exploring the former prison cells, heard a whisper in his ear. The spectral voice muttered the words, 'I didn't do it.' Startled, the visitor turned around only to find the cell empty.

In the later years of its operation, the prison transitioned into a Category B prison and held some of the UK's most notorious criminals. It subsequently became a venue for various macabre entertainments, ghost tours and investigations, with the reputation of being one of Gloucester's most haunted locations. In the prison's old wing many have claimed to see ghostly figures walking down the deserted hallways, or to feel they are being watched, or to glimpse the sight of a shadowy form slipping away into the darkness.

The prison became a site for public executions in the nineteenth century. Notorious hangman William Calcraft, known for his long tenure and brutal execution methods, carried out many of these hangings. On 18 November 2023, the site hosted a 'Dark Tourism' Christmas fair. As at the time of writing, the prison hosts a variety of events with public access, including guided tours and ghost hunts.

Blackfriars Priory

Built in 1239 on land formerly occupied by Gloucester Castle using funds and materials donated by Henry III, this priory was the home of a very popular order of Dominican black friars for 300 years. It now stands as one of the oldest surviving medieval Dominican priories in England. Having undergone many changes during the centuries following the Dissolution (the first of which was conversion into a Tudor mansion by wealthy merchant and local alderman Thomas Bell), in 1956 it drew the attention of the Ministry of Works. The Ministry began buying bits of it back piecemeal, and in 1960 the property came 'under guardianship', at which time all post-medieval floors and partitions were removed. In more recent times, restoration work has uncovered a dungeon. This discovery is linked to the appearance of a hooded figure who hovers nearby.

The priory is renowned for its stunning 'scissor-braced' roof in the dormitory, using timbers donated from the royal forests by Henry III, and also the magnificent Scriptorium, the oldest purpose-built library in Britain. Here, the friars would sit by windows carefully angled to allow light to fall on their desks; they studied, wrote sermons, illustrated manuscripts – and doodled. This is evidenced by the medieval engraving of a lady's face in the stonework by one of the windows. It's not known whether this might have been 'a lady of the night' of whom the friar was dreaming, or the Virgin Mary!

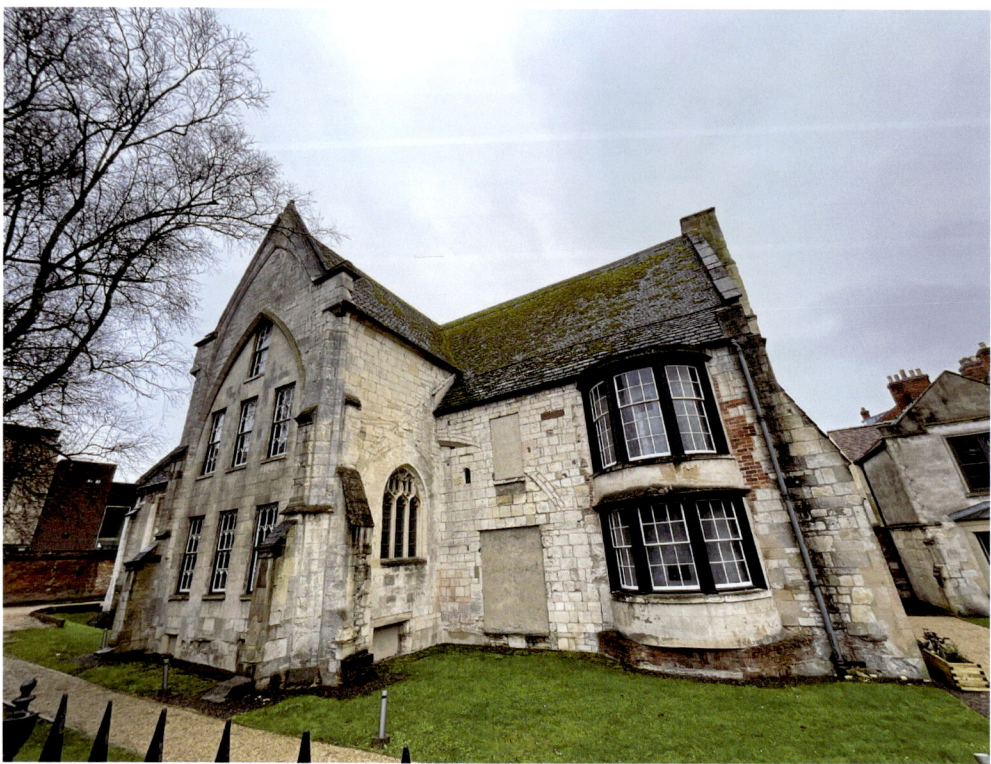

Blackfriars, Gloucester. (Courtesy of Jamie Robinson)

The black friars were greatly valued by the community they served, as they mingled with the populace offering healing, counselling and spiritual direction, in those times when they weren't being required to attend eight services a day of the Divine Office. Present-day visitors have reported eerie encounters with shadowy friars, who have been sighted wandering the priory's ancient halls, particularly in the late hours of the evening. The priory is also known for unexplained auditory phenomena. Visitors report hearing the distinct sound of Gregorian chanting, without any visible source for the music.

The New Inn, Northgate Street

The New Inn's fine galleried courtyard, bar and accommodation has been the scene of diverse human activity for 560 years and has a full share of ghost stories. It was originally built in 1455 as a pilgrim inn to house visitors to the shrine of King Edward II in St Peter's Abbey. In the sixteenth century strolling minstrels were popular and plays were staged in the courtyard, some of which, it is said, were performed by William Shakespeare and his troupe.

Strange sounds and unexplained 'whisperings' have been recorded in the cellar, whilst some claim to feel the presence of a 'bad-tempered spirit' there. CCTV cameras have captured an unattended pint glass mysteriously disappearing. Kitchen staff report the sight of pots and pans flying around whenever the kitchen is left untidy.

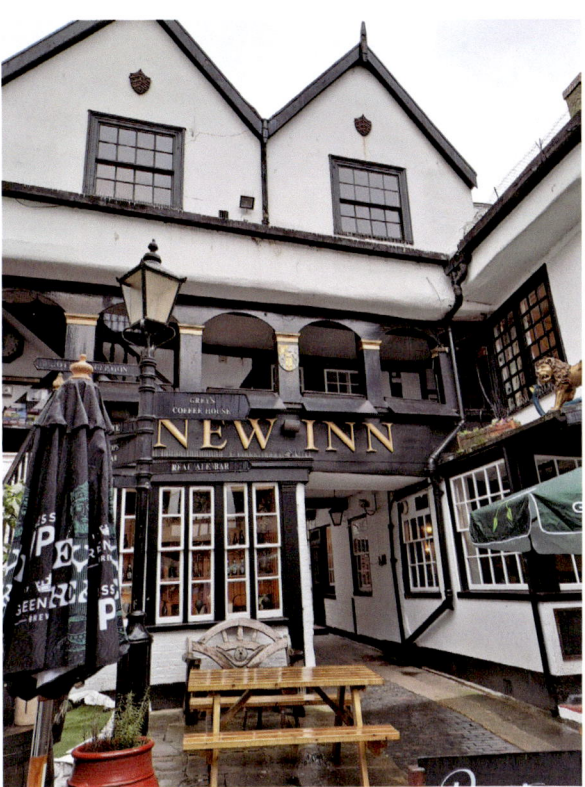

Courtyard of the New Inn, Gloucester.

A sign outside the inn proudly announces it as 'the most haunted pub in Gloucester' and among its numerous unearthly residents, visitors are invited to look out for:

> The Old Lady in Black Sitting in the Restaurant; Two Children Playing in the Courtyard; The Old Man Who Drops his Pint in the Bar; and The Bogey Man Behind the Bedroom Door.

During the Reformation in the sixteenth century, the inn served as a secret meeting place for Catholic priests. In the 1800s it became a popular social hub. Today, the New Inn stands as the most complete surviving example of a medieval courtyard inn in England. An oft-repeated tale at the inn centres upon the spirit of a woman who tragically lost her life at the inn centuries ago. Visitors and staff alike have reported seeing her as she wanders the inn's corridors late at night. She vanishes as suddenly as she appears, leaving a lingering sense of sadness behind her. However, other guests have reported hearing the faint sound of laughter and merriment at times when the bar is closed to present-day customers.

The Folk of Gloucester

This beautiful timber-framed building on Westgate Street is one of the oldest buildings in Gloucester and dates from 1500. Previously known as the Gloucester Folk Museum, it opened under its present name in 2019. It is thought Bishop Hooper spent his final

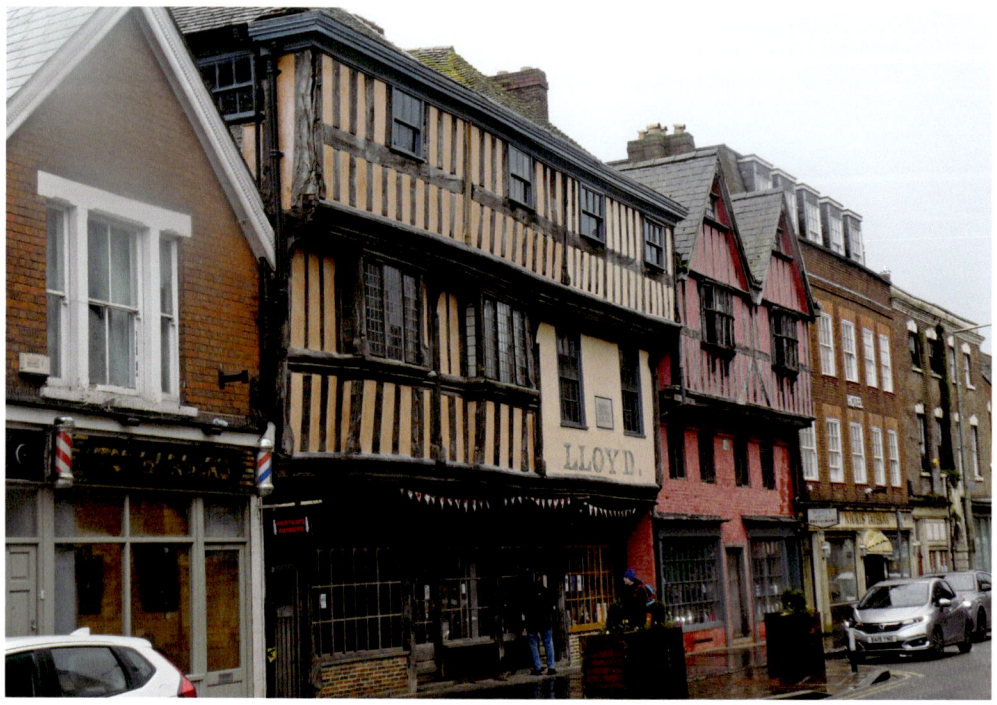

View of the Folk from across the road, Gloucester. (Courtesy of Jamie Robinson)

night here before his public execution. Amongst the uncanny experiences reported in the building, some visitors describe a vision of the Pin Factory Ghost, from the time when The Folk was used as a pin factory. This shadowy worker is observed labouring away, replicating the rhythmic movements of pin-making, and is especially visible during nighttime events. Also regularly reported is the figure of a Tudor-era merchant, believed to be a former resident of the house, who has been seen wandering the halls, seemingly lost in thought or in search of something.

The building has throughout the centuries served various purposes from the time that Tudor merchant called it home. Now it houses displays which capture the essence of Gloucester's cultural heritage. Original medieval wall paintings have been partially uncovered in one of the rooms, and visitors may see a unique original drawing of a young King Henry VIII playing the harp. One of the most poignant exhibits is the charred stump believed to be part of the stake at which Bishop John Hooper was burned. This stump was discovered during excavations in St Mary's Square to provide a foundation for the bishop's monument facing the cathedral.

At night, uncanny experiences intensify in this building; those watching historical re-enactments feel a sudden, unexplained chill in the air and an eerie sensation of being watched, while disembodied voices have been heard echoing through the empty rooms.

2

Cheltenham and Surrounds

No more, you petty spirits of region low,
Offend our hearing; hush!

Cymbeline, Act 5, Scene 4

It is easy to characterise Cheltenham as a Regency spa town, yet its history dates back many centuries earlier and curious stories emerge from several locations. Cheltenham features in the earliest pages of the Gloucestershire section of the Domesday Book and was awarded a market charter in 1226. One of the most notable phantoms originated in this town: the Morton Case seems to have served as one of the inspirations for Susan Hill in her story *The Woman in Black*.

The Old Restoration, Nos 55–57 High Street

This building, with its beautiful, elaborate inn sign, dates back to the 1600s. A customer reports sighting the disquieting image of a young girl mysteriously floating

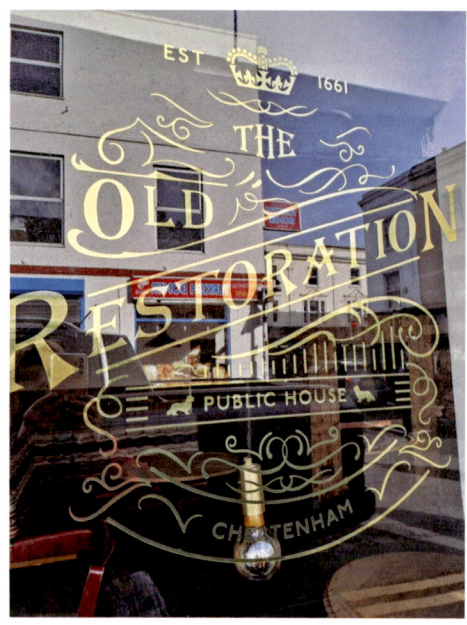

The Old Restoration, Cheltenham.

along the corridor upstairs. Staff also maintain that in a particular room items simply disappear for months on end, then reappear.

Everyman Theatre, Regent Street

Most actors admit to a belief in unusual rituals in order to ensure a good performance on stage free of mishaps. Actors, directors, ushers, theatregoers and front-of-house staff are all included among the phantoms said to roam the theatres of England which they loved so much during their lifetimes. The Everyman Theatre is no exception. Reports mention a 'ghost dressed in a 1940s suit' seen during the renovation of the theatre. The *Gloucestershire Echo* described the experience of builder Walter Charnock whilst he was busy working on the theatre's restoration project in 2011. He encountered a figure leaning on a banister, but within thirty seconds, it vanished. Unexplained music has also been heard within the building with no apparent cause and no musicians playing; this has been reported independently by several people, including a long-serving technician. The music is most often heard by those near the main auditorium doors in the foyer.

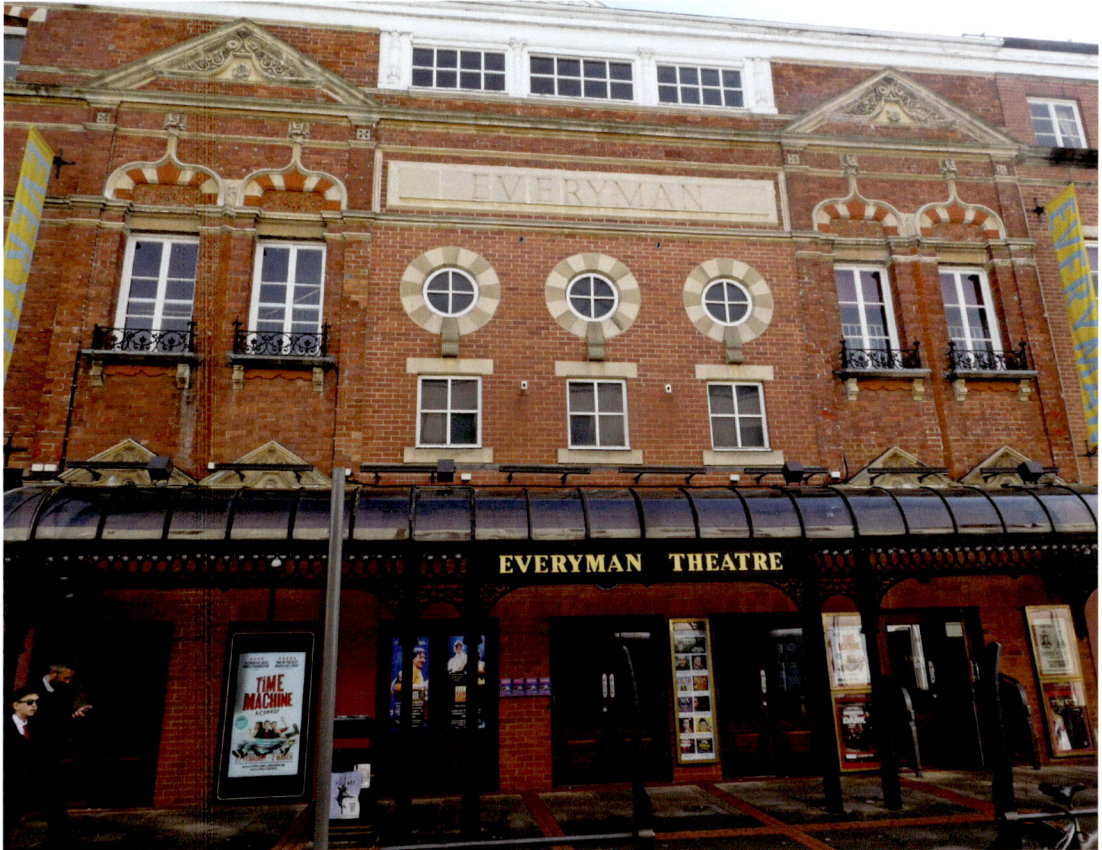

Everyman Theatre, Cheltenham. (Courtesy of Jamie Robinson)

The Old Courthouse, County Court Road

This grand building no longer serves its former function but has been converted into a restaurant, and I visited when it was Jamie's Italian. The restaurant employees have heard several eerie tales and experienced odd events in the building, particularly in the basement. Customers would report an uncanny feeling downstairs where the guest toilets are situated; I would agree with that, having experienced it myself. Two customers described the ghostly image of a young boy. Staff have also, in the past, been told to avoid the judge's chair as it is believed that a couple of former judges died of a heart attack while sitting in it.

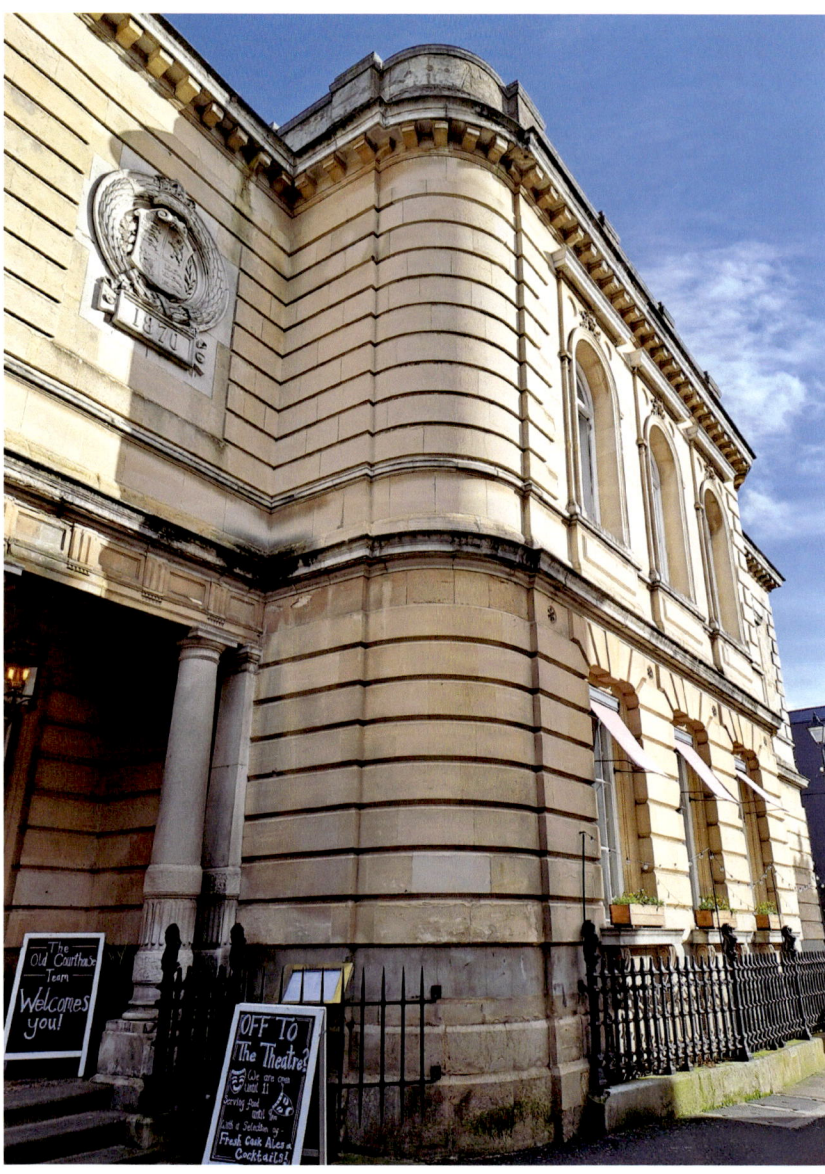

The Old Courthouse, Cheltenham.

Montpellier Terrace

Montpellier is one of the most historic areas of Cheltenham. The famous spa waters were discovered here long before it was named after the French city, and its streets and walks follow the same routes as the Regency promenades. Any trace of the original Royal Well Spa and Old Well Walk have been buried under such developments as Cheltenham Ladies College. Shops and businesses quickly sprang up to meet the demands of the many health and pleasure-seekers flocking to the town in the early 1800s.

Residents of a house in elegant Montpellier Terrace tell of disembodied voices, footsteps and inexplicable noises, and some have claimed to feel they are 'being followed by shadowy toad-like creatures crawling out from under the bed and flying straight through the skirting board'. Kelly lives in a flat here, and says she saw the spectre of a man outside her bathroom. She has also experienced doors locking on their own, the smell of pipe smoke, and coats inexplicably falling onto the floor.

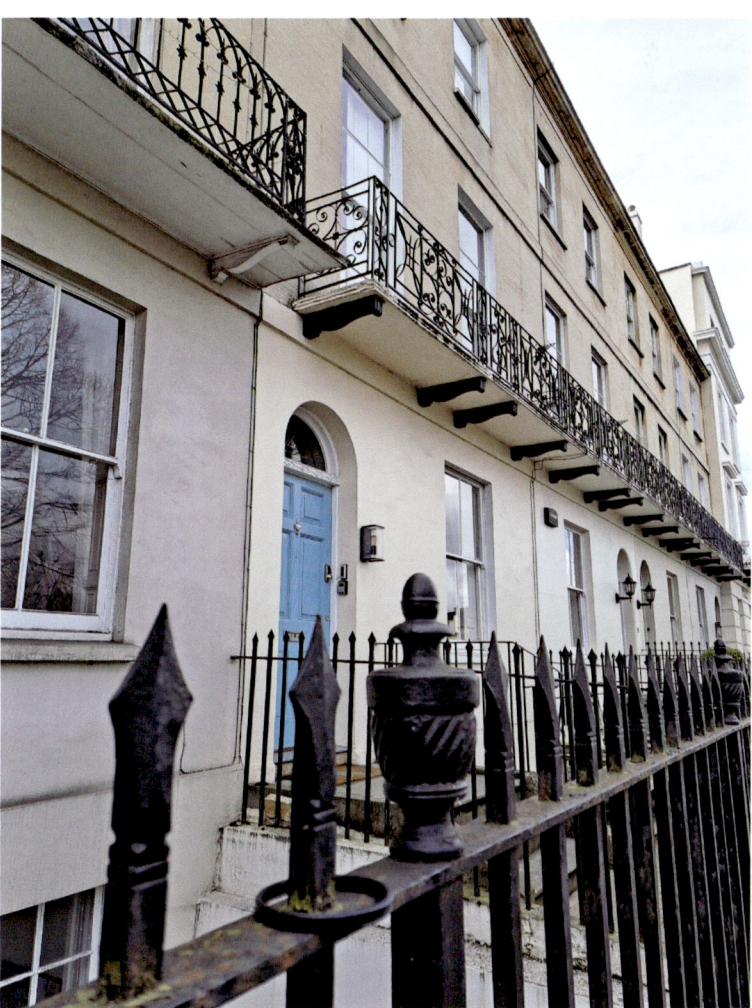

Montpellier Terrace, Cheltenham.

Rotunda (now the Ivy), Montpellier Street

The original Montpellier Spa Rotunda building built in the nineteenth century still exists, now housing the Ivy restaurant and retaining many of its original features and also the impressive dome. The building houses one of the main wells serving the famous Cheltenham medicinal waters, and it was converted into a restaurant in 2017. Prior to its transformation into the Ivy brasserie, the building was a Lloyds Bank. Uncanny activity first began at that time: the bank employees reported eerie experiences and felt as if 'a spiritual figure was always watching them'.

I can confirm that the interior of the dome above the distinctive Ivy bar conveys 'a sense of presence' quite apart from any atmosphere created by those who throng the brasserie below. I can well imagine how the staff here may have felt when this was a grand banking hall.

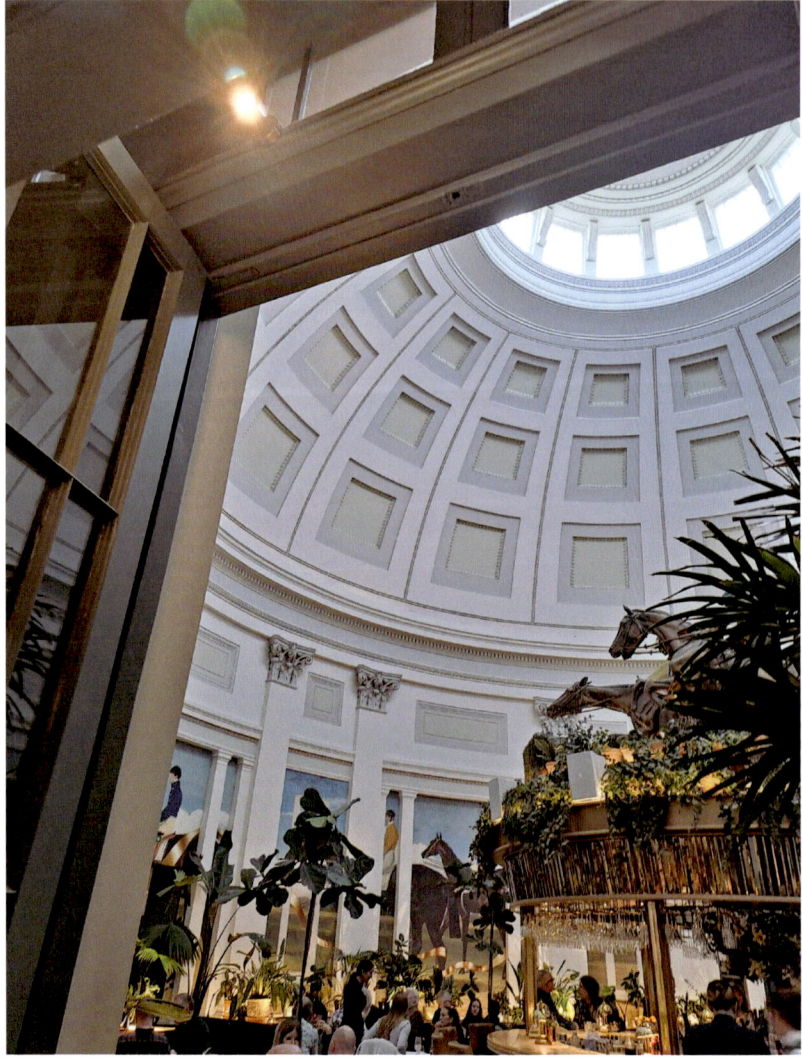

Inside the Ivy, Cheltenham.

St Anne's House, Pittville Circus Road

This property was built in the 1860s and named Garden Reach; its first residents were Henry and Elizabeth Swinhoe and their family. When Elizabeth, Henry's beloved wife, gave birth to a stillborn child and died in 1866, Henry was heartbroken and took to drink to deal with his pain. Later, he married Imogen, from Clifton in Bristol. But their relationship was tumultuous from the beginning and marred by conflict. Imogen, too, took to drinking, and it is said Henry ill-treated her. In 1876 they decided to separate. Imogen went back to Clifton and in July that year, Henry died at Garden Reach. Imogen died in September 1878 in Clifton her body transported back to Cheltenham where she was buried in the grounds of Holy Trinity Church.

The next owner of the property, Benjamin Littlewood, renovated the house and renamed it Pittville House. He died not long afterwards, in September, in the same room as Henry Swinhoe had. In 1882 the Despard family moved in; subsequently Captain Despard's servants, children and guests all claimed to see the wraith that later became known as the Cheltenham Ghost. Many have detected strong similarities between these encounters, and the description of the 'evil, vengeful spectre' who stalks the pages of Susan Hill's book *The Woman in Black*.

The true-life case at Garden Reach was reported to F. W. Myers of the Society for Psychical Research by Rosina, one of Captain Despard's daughters, who initially followed the time-honoured custom of claiming to be 'a friend of a friend' of the family. The case was the society's first major investigation and one of the most detailed of the late nineteenth century. At first Rosina chose the pseudonym of R. C. Morton, so the story became known as 'the Morton Case'. In December 1884 Rosina, nineteen

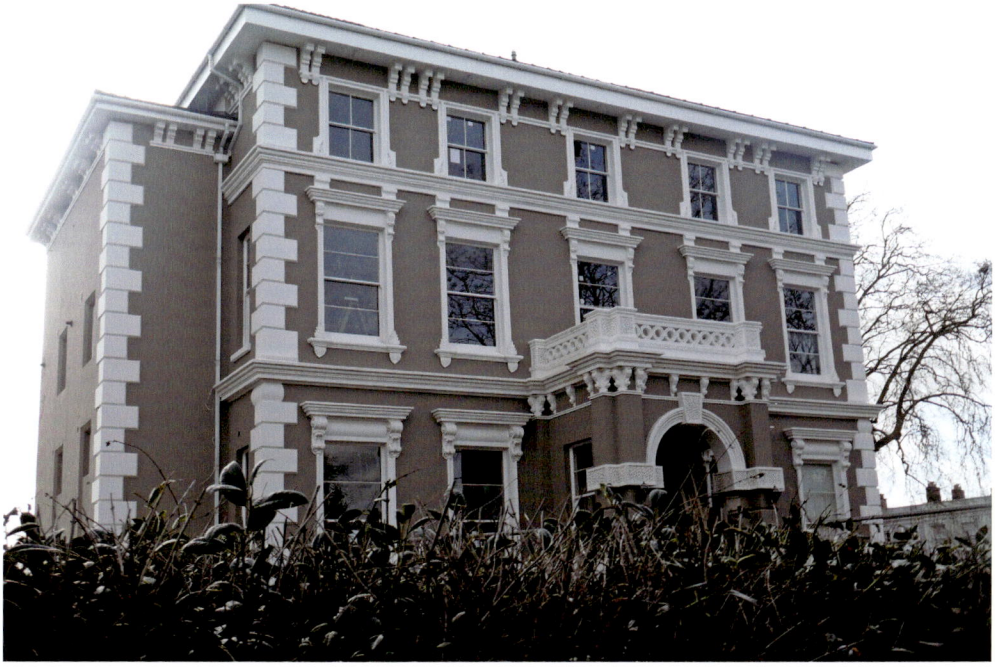

St Anne's House, Pittville Circus Road, Cheltenham. (Courtesy of Jamie Robinson)

years old, who by that time had chosen to reveal her true identity, gave the following testimony to Frederic Myers, the Honourable Secretary of the Society:

> I had gone up to my room but was not yet in bed when I heard someone at the door and thinking it might be my mother, on opening the door I saw no one, but on going further along the passage I saw a tall lady dressed in black standing at the head of the stairs.
>
> After a few moments she descended the stairs and I followed for a short distance feeling curious as to who it could be. I had only a small piece of candle and it suddenly burned itself out. Being unable to see clearly I went back to my room.
>
> The figure was a tall lady dressed in what seemed to be soft black woollen material and when she moved her face was hidden by a handkerchief held in her right hand.
>
> This is all I noticed then but on further occasions when I was able to observe her more closely I saw that her left hand was nearly hidden by her sleeve and a Widow's cuff was visible on both wrists. The whole impression was that of a lady in widow's weeds.

Rosina claimed to see the lady about a dozen times and occasionally tried to speak to her. Rosina was convinced she attempted to reply but all she heard was a sigh and the ghost disappeared into the darkness. On other occasions the family heard mysterious bangs, bumps and the turning of door handles by invisible hands. These sightings continued and were corroborated by Rosina's siblings, servants and neighbours who had seen the apparition even in broad daylight, occasionally mistaking her for a living person. The sightings were most frequent in the months of July, August and September; these were the three months on which Henry, and Imogen, and Benjamin Littlewood had died.

On one occasion Rosina was in a room with her pregnant sister, Frederica, when she saw the mournful black-garbed lady just behind Frederica. Frederica lost her baby a few weeks later. It may be that element of the story had its unconscious influence on Susan Hill; every appearance of her fictional 'woman in black' is followed by the death of a child in the local community.

Some believed the spectre to be that of Imogen Swinhoe, perhaps returning to resentfully watch the family who seemed so much happier than she had been in that house. She was seen less during 1887 to 1889 and not seen again by the Despards from 1892, the year before they moved out. After Benjamin Littlewood's period of ownership, the property became a boarding school for boys in the 1900s, but the school was forced to move into new premises because of regular appearance of the ghost. After that, the property was occupied as a nunnery for a period of time, and final converted into separate residences.

However, in 1970, a woman taking a driving test stopped abruptly outside the property to avoid a woman in black who she said was crossing the road; when she explained this to the driving instructor, he said that he had not seen the woman. A few years later, one night at 10 p.m., two men saw 'a strange looking woman in a thick black Victorian dress on the footpath' very close by.

The property is now known as St Anne's House and no further uncanny tales have emerged from this area since, but many years after the Despard family's time a full review of the case was published, and investigations completed as recently as 2021.

Belas Knap Long Barrow, Cleeve Hill

These that I bring unto their latest home,
With burial amongst their ancestors.

Titus Andronicus, Act 1, Scene 1

This impressive burial site is located beyond fields reached by a steep climb signposted from a minor road off the A46. The area is well known for its unearthly atmosphere. The site lies a 2-mile walk uphill and has several small enclosed entrances containing ancient stones. Skeletons of a chieftain and his family were found in one of the burial chambers during excavations some years ago. This location frequently fills visitors with a strong sense of awe: 'One can feel the ancient mystery embedded in the Cotswold hills.'

One visitor, Gemma, provides this account:

My partner and I visited Belas Knap one evening last autumn. On the way up … I felt a presence in the woods, along with one close behind me that felt as though it might have been a priest. We both also felt a strange pins-and-needles sensation, and an inward chill.

On reaching the barrow we sat inside the main burial chamber and relaxed… We'd been there for maybe half an hour just chatting when the pins-and-needles feeling hit us both again. It was so powerful that my limbs were actually vibrating. We then heard slow, rhythmic drums that seemed to come from outside the chamber… no sound could reach the barrow from the road even on a calm night. The drums didn't fade away as you would expect them to had they come from a passing car; they just suddenly stopped. I felt that we were being warned off, so we left. I didn't feel 'normal' again until we were back on the road.

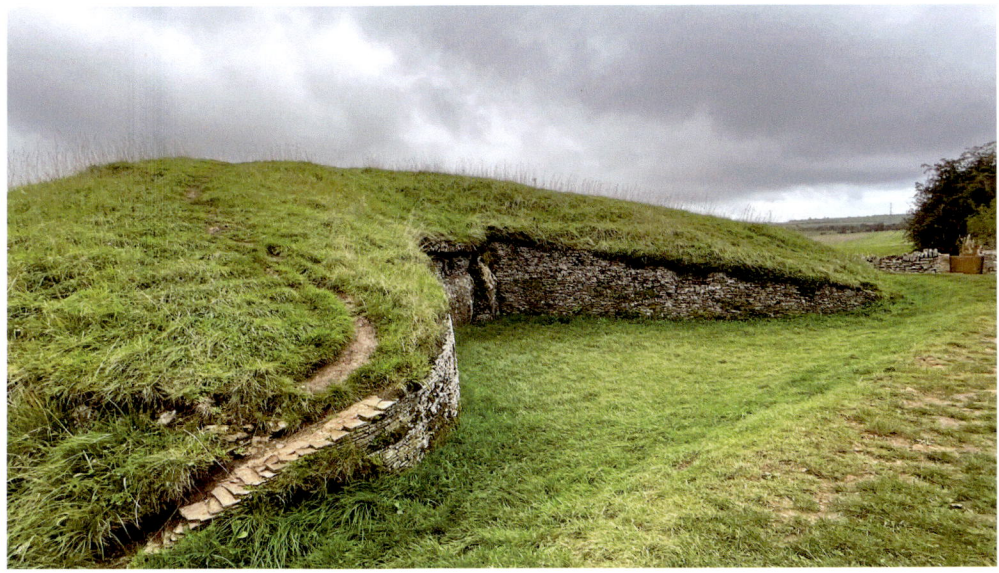

Belas Knap. (Courtesy of Jamie Robinson)

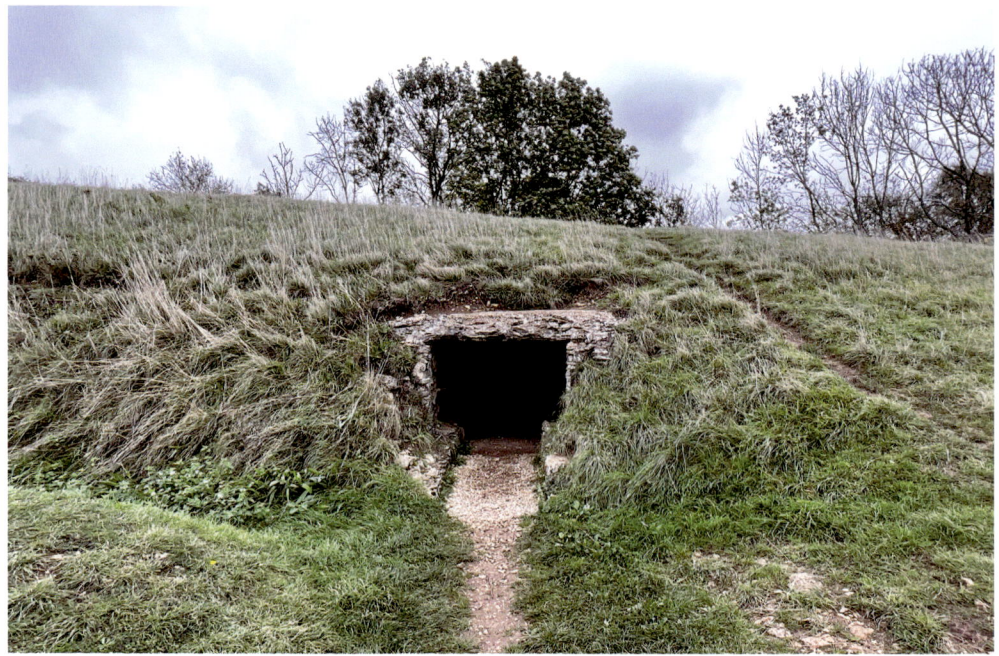

Side chamber entrance, Belas Knap. (Courtesy of Jamie Robinson)

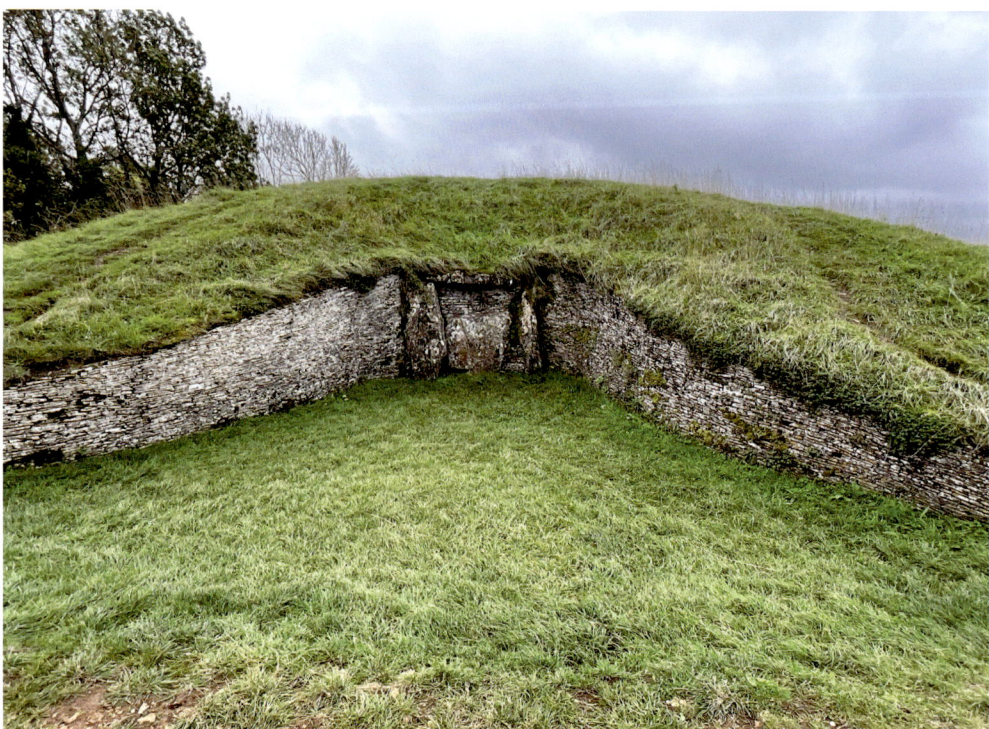

False entrance, Belas Knap. (Courtesy of Jamie Robinson)

The Village of Prestbury

Frighting her pale-faced villages

Richard II, Act 2, Scene 3

The pretty little village of Prestbury, north-east of Cheltenham, is considered one of 'the most haunted in the UK' and many villagers report uncanny events.

The Plough Inn, Mill Street

Located opposite St Mary's Church, the Plough Inn is a Grade II listed seventeenth-century pub around which a number of mysterious tales circulate, both inside the building and on the road outside. A former landlady reports that one morning she came downstairs to find all the furniture had been rearranged and stacked up in one room. Patrons and staff of the inn have testified to hearing horses' hooves running through the building. Others see a kindly old man wearing a hat and an old tweed jacket who sits in a corner with a smile then vanishes as quickly as he appeared.

Around the village, inside houses, inns, hotels, and out on the roads, stories seem to emerge from every period: medieval times, the Wars of the Roses, the English Civil War, the 1700s, 1800s and even the 1970s.

One episode associated with the time of the Civil War centres upon Mill Street. During that time a royal dispatch rider was riding from Sudeley Castle to Gloucester.

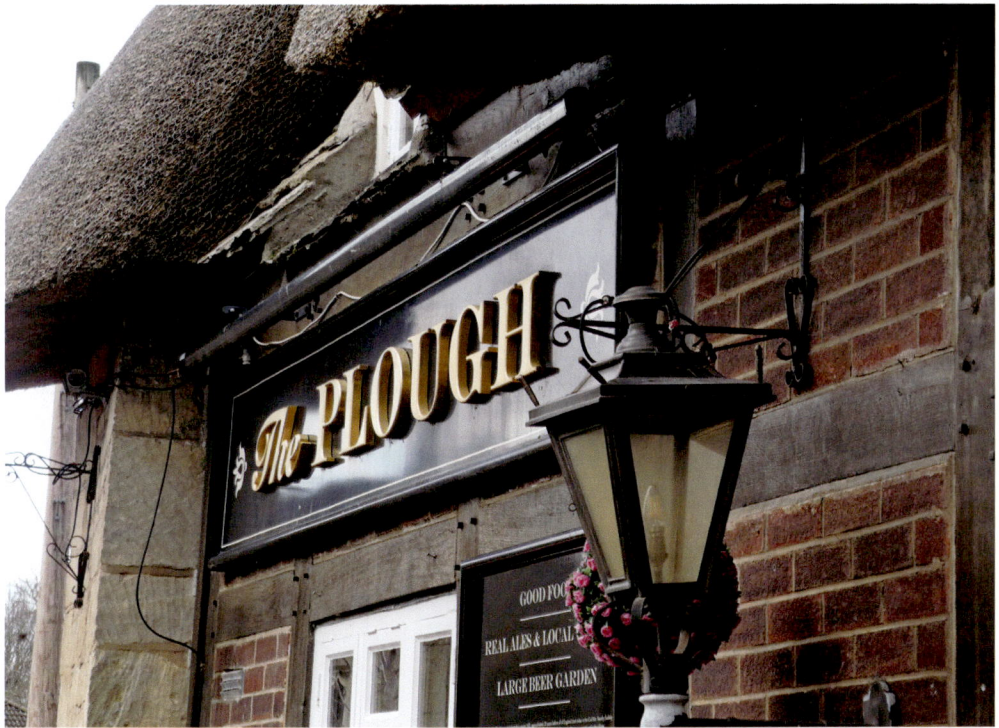

The Plough Inn, Prestbury. (Courtesy of Jamie Robinson)

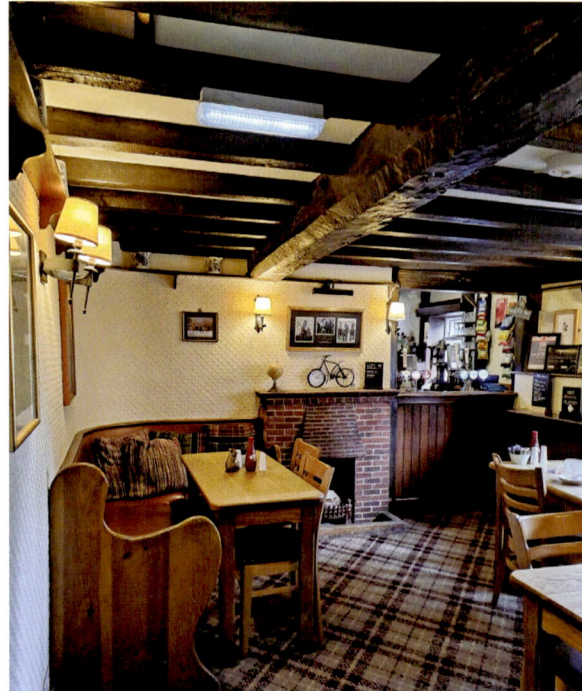

Interior of the bar at the Plough Inn, Prestbury.

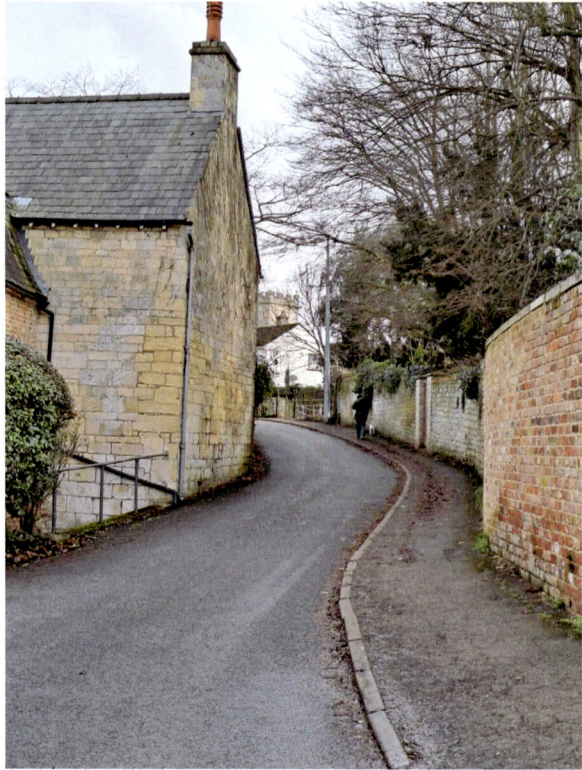

Mill Street, Prestbury.

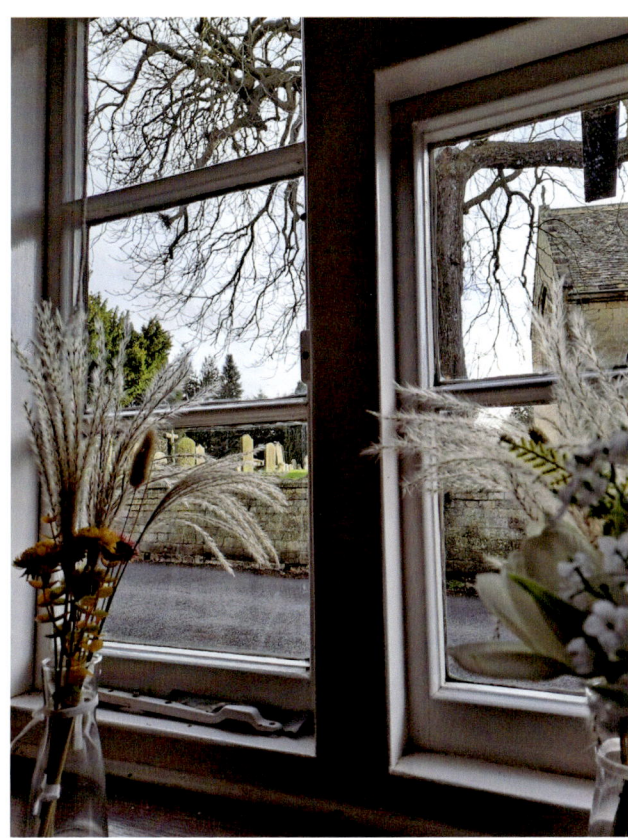

View out to Mill Street from inside the Plough, Prestbury.

The Roundheads of Prestbury stretched a rope across the road, knocking the Cavalier rider off his horse and then executed him. The ghostly outline of horse and rider accompanied by the sound of horses' hooves have been reported on more than one occasion, appearing 'out of thin air' and galloping at full speed down the street.

Another account of invisible horses' hooves centres upon the area of Mill Street outside the Plough. A local postman reports that he often heard this sound behind him as he reached the inn. He would pull over to the church wall to let the horses pass, but then the sound would stop and no horses would appear. It is also said that sheep are reluctant to be herded past this section of Mill Street and that dogs and horses, too, have reacted, with some known to 'freeze to the spot'.

The King's Arms, High Street

Curious events are reported outside the King's Arms. Several claim to have seen the hooded phantom in long black robe who walks past the pub at Christmas, Easter and All Hallows' Eve. This was also the location for an uncanny experience that took place in the 1970s. At that time on Gold Cup Night a group of four women in front of the pub saw a man standing opposite on the curb waiting to cross the road. He was dressed as a jockey with a peaked cap, and began to cross the road, but disappeared halfway across and was then seen crossing the road again round the corner.

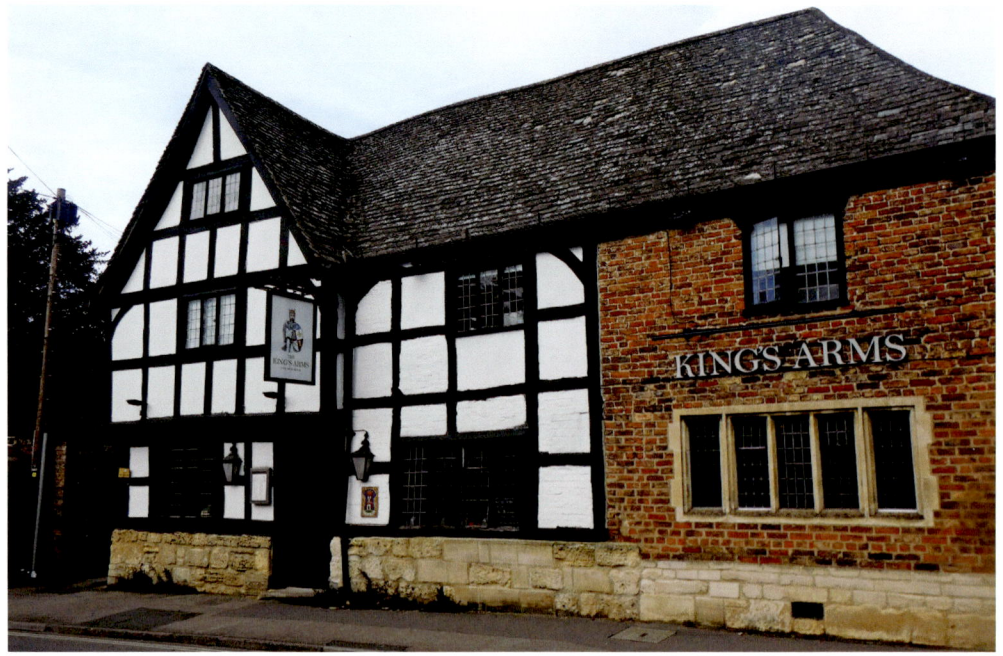

King's Arms, Prestbury. (Courtesy of Jamie Robinson)

Around the Village

A number of residents can offer their own disquieting tales. A new resident reported noticing a Cavalier soldier in one of the streets; but although she was with her husband at the time, he insisted he saw nothing. The former Prestbury House Hotel has also seen strange events. It is known that during the English Civil War, Charles I's messenger rode up to the hotel to deliver a message and fell prey to his enemies there; his head was severed from his body. Today some report that his galloping steed can be heard. He is not the only horseman to have met his fate in the village in the past. Reports tell of the Charging Horseman who appears riding his white horse at Easter and Christmas and is rumoured to have been killed by a Lancastrian arrow during the Wars of the Roses.

Snowshill

> Peep through thy marble mansion; help;
> Or we poor ghosts will cry
> To the shining synod of the rest

Cymbeline, Act 5, Scene 4

The village of Snowshill, among the hills near Broadway, was once owned by Winchcombe Abbey, 8 miles away. The abbey was first built in 798 by King Kenulf of Mercia as a nunnery; nearly 200 years later it was re-founded as a Benedictine community and became one of the most powerful Benedictine monasteries in England until its dissolution in 1539. But, as the ghost stories of England often testify, you cannot stop a monk by dissolving his monastery. Some of them seem to have lingered for hundreds of years, and they make their presence known at various locations in Snowshill.

Between 1969 and 1979, the landlord of the Snowshill Arms, Alastair Biles, frequently sighted a ghostly hooded figure in the ancient upstairs part of the inn who could open doors and send his dog running downstairs to the newer part of the building. The unearthly visitor would sometimes take a very distinct form, but at other times appeared as a misty shape that would disappear through walls or closed doors. Despite his dog's reaction, Alastair reported that neither he nor his family found this figure threatening.

Reactions to the shadowy monk vary, though, among those who have seen him within sixteenth-century Snowshill Manor close by, and in the lane that runs past. Located on the steep side of a spectacular valley, Snowshill Manor is renowned for its most eccentric owner, the great collector Charles Wade (1883–1956), who researched the ghosts he sensed in his home.

Charles discovered the house in a semi-derelict state in 1919, fell in love with it and immediately put in a successful offer. He entrusted the extensive repairs and renovations to a foreman, W. A. Lewin, who was of the same heart and mind: 'I hear the subdued whisperings of the spirits which haunt the house … when you return you will feel the atmosphere of their visit radiating from the panels in the dining room, and elsewhere.'

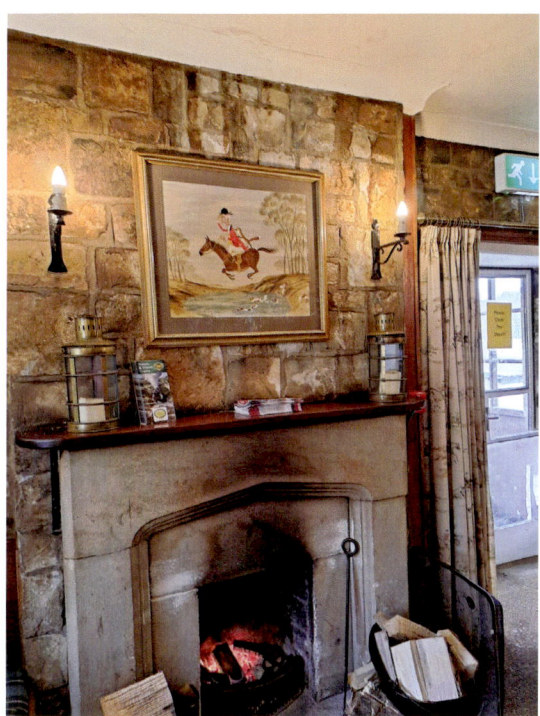

Inside the bar of the Snowshill Arms, Snowshill.

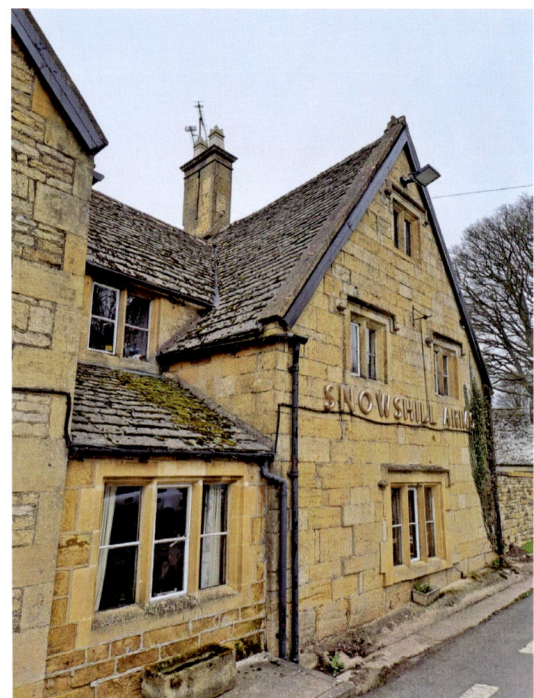

Snowshill Arms exterior.

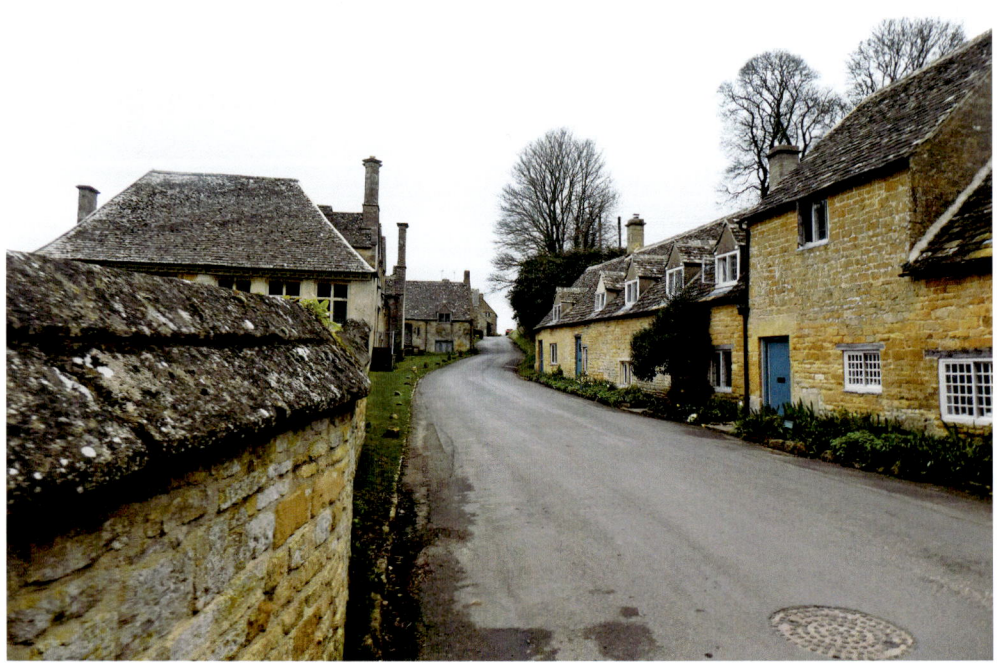

The lane past Snowshill Manor. (Courtesy of Jamie Robinson)

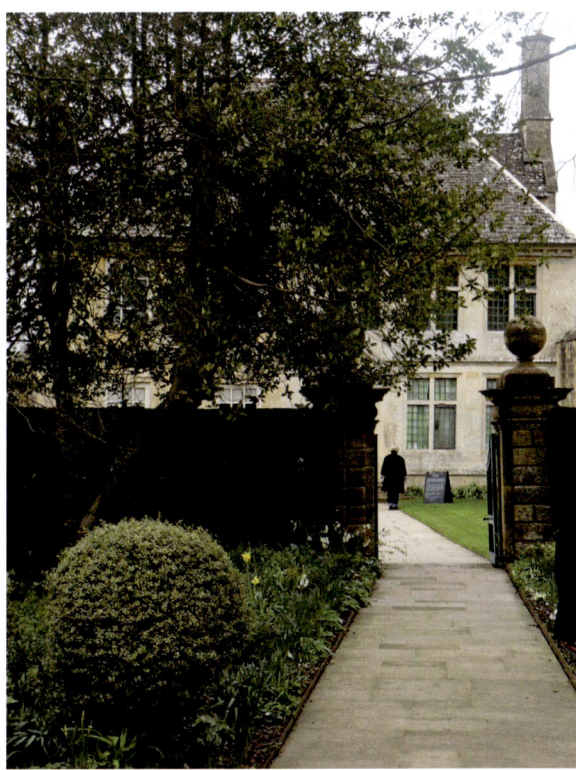

Snowshill Manor. (Courtesy of Jamie Robinson)

Charles was a highly creative man who loved to dress up in numerous theatrical costumes, but for day-to-day wear his preference was eighteenth-century garb. As author Jonathan Howard says in his book A Thousand Fancies: 'Charles was noted for unparalleled eccentricity and bohemian dress. He was commonly seen in a winged collar, with bow tie, dark waistcoat, single-breasted wool jacket, and matching knee breeches, met by ribbed woollen socks rising from his leather brogues.'

Charles became a familiar figure around the antique shops of Cheltenham, Broadway and other Cotswold towns, buying new items that took his fancy, and adding them to the displays in his already packed house.

Every room is devoted to his idiosyncratic collection, which many visitors enjoy, but one I spoke to considered 'creepy'. Charles himself moved into the former priest's house in the courtyard, where he followed a quaint and anachronistic lifestyle, whilst still spending many hours inside the manor house transforming it into a unique testimony to his vision. One of his ghostly companions was the previously mentioned Benedictine monk of Winchcombe Abbey, who has appeared to staff and visitors both inside and in the vicinity of the house.

Charles gave instructions for the addition of mysterious doors 'to invite questions about what lay beyond' and insisted that 'patina from age' be conserved 'a tangible link with the many spirits in the manor'. He built two stone spiral staircases and 'engaged up to twenty-eight workmen … many of whom slept in the attics during the week. For one, the first night was the last. He had a visitation from the ghost of a Benedictine monk which village tradition spoke of haunting the manor'.

Despite their experience of eerie events in and around the manor house, the local villagers liked Charles very much, and in 1951 (the year when he transferred the property and its collection to the National Trust), others saw him as 'mischievous, waxy complexioned, a medieval face seen through the woodsmoke'. After his death, Charles was buried with his mother and sisters in Snowshill churchyard.

Sudeley Castle

> This castle hath a pleasant seat
>
> *Macbeth*, Act 1, Scene 6

Sudeley Castle was built in 1442 in Winchcombe on the remains of a twelfth-century castle. It has played host to many historical figures over the centuries and – according to staff, visitors and guests – numerous ghosts too. They have been sighted or felt in the castle corridors, in a number of chambers including the Chandos Room and the Leather Bedroom, and within the castle's ruined tithe barn.

The castle's present chatelaine, Elizabeth, Lady Ashcombe, has been at the castle for over fifty years and although she says she has never seen any of the ghosts herself, she has this story to recount:

> My sister Genie was staying one Christmas in the Leather Bedroom. She woke to a figure in the doorway, coming out of a very bright white light with a dark hat, long dark hair, and wearing a kind of uniform. He looked like a Cavalier, maybe from the Civil War. He sat down at the dressing table and turned around; at that point, she fled the room, screaming.

The Crown has held the castle during several different periods in history, but the most frequent unearthly sighting is that of a former housekeeper known as Janet who was devoted to the castle. The 'Haunted Staircase' on the visitors' tour route honours Janet's numerous appearances.

Janet worked at the castle in the late nineteenth and early twentieth century. She ensured the house stayed in perfect order, and also felt it her duty to protect the honour of the young housemaids. She would station herself at the top of the staircase leading to their bedroom well into the night, to ensure no youthful manservant gained access. Those who see her claim she was aware of their presence and frantically shooed them away, waving a feather duster to make her more intimidating. The apparition is frequently sitting or standing guard at the top of the staircase.

Janet's task is particularly ironic as one of the other stories told of Sudeley Castle is that of the attempted seduction of young Princess Elizabeth by Sir Thomas Seymour. Sir Thomas married Queen Katherine Parr after the death of her husband Henry VIII. In the case of the young princess, no such vigilant maidservant as Janet stood guard to protect her from the advances of the nefarious Sir Thomas. Historical novelists have found rich fodder for their fictional speculations as to what actually happened in that chamber. Sir Thomas later had his come-uppance when he was executed for treason.

The castle is most renowned for being Katherine's last home, and some claim to have seen her phantom too. She was an intelligent woman who had a strong interest in

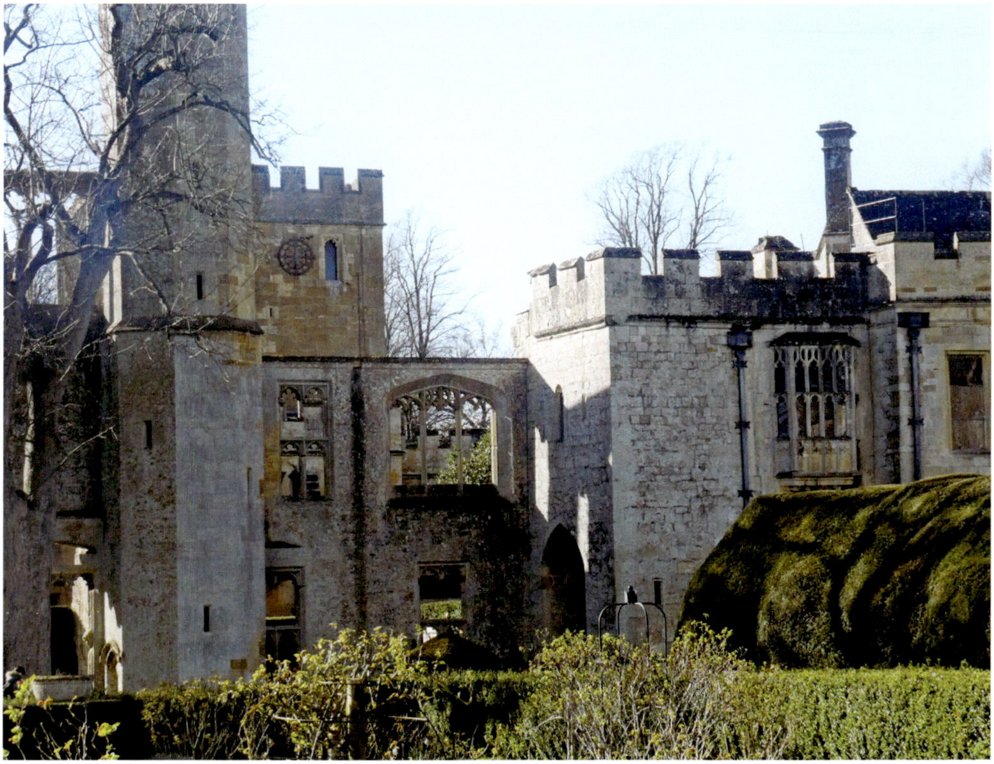

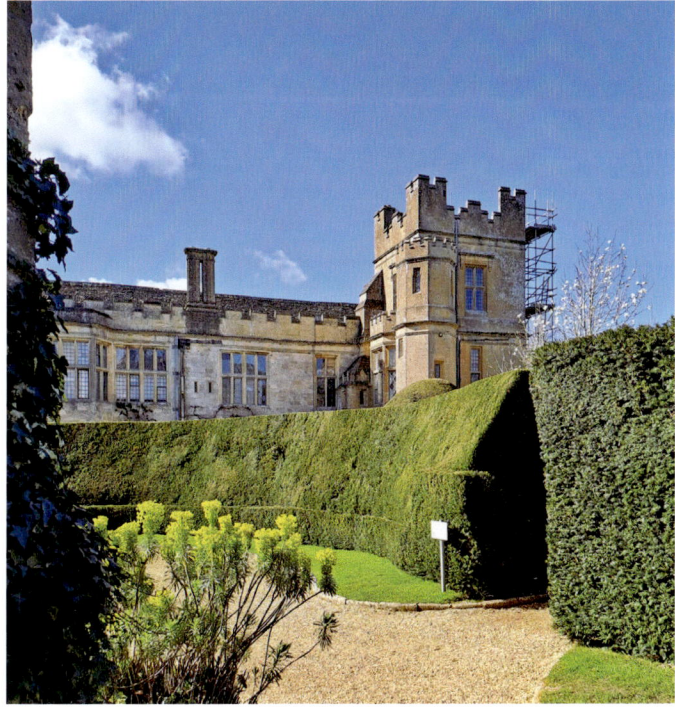

Above and right: Sudeley Castle. (Courtesy of Jamie Robinson)

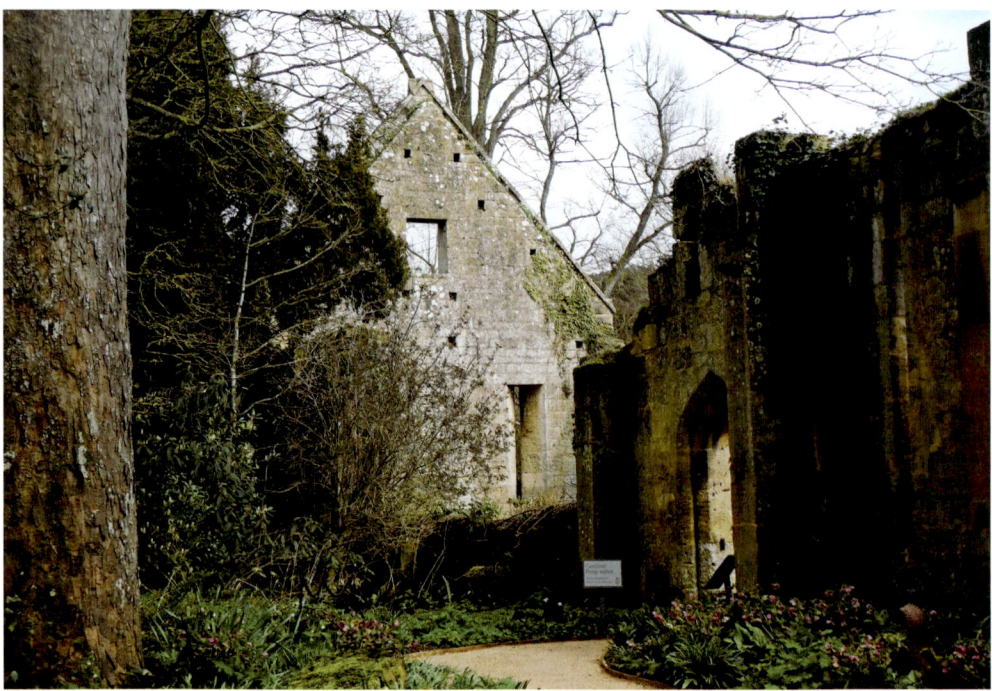

Ruins of a tithe barn at Sudeley Castle. (Courtesy of Jamie Robinson)

religious reform, and skilfully negotiated the dangerous mood swings of Henry in his final years. She also wrote the first book published in England by a woman under her own name and in the English language. But Katherine made one major mistake after surviving Henry: she went on to marry Sir Thomas. Sadly, she did not survive the birth of her baby Mary, about whom history knows nothing beyond the first two years of her life. Katherine's funeral and burial took place in the castle chapel (now known as St Mary's Church), with Lady Jane Grey serving as the chief mourner. It was the first Protestant funeral held in the English language.

Katherine's remains were treated with disrespect in subsequent centuries, when those discovering her lead coffin in the now-ruined chapel thought they should open it up to check that the inscription was true. Ultimately, in April 1861 the chapel was restored and re-dedicated as St Mary's Church, and Katherine's remains now lie with dignity beneath a simple white effigy upon a new tomb.

In the church I felt a strong atmosphere, as if the recorded visitations of Katherine's shadowy form are connected with the earlier desecration of her resting place. Certainly, her presence in the house disturbed one of those ghoulish people who robbed her coffin. He immediately linked the two events, felt remorseful, and tried to make reparation by returning the item to her coffin.

Sir Thomas disappeared from the castle straight after Katherine's death without even waiting for her funeral, to continue courting the Princess Elizabeth. He also tried his luck with the Princess Mary. He met his fate the next year on the orders of King Edward VI. At the news of his execution Elizabeth is said to have remarked, 'This day died a man with much wit and very little judgement.'

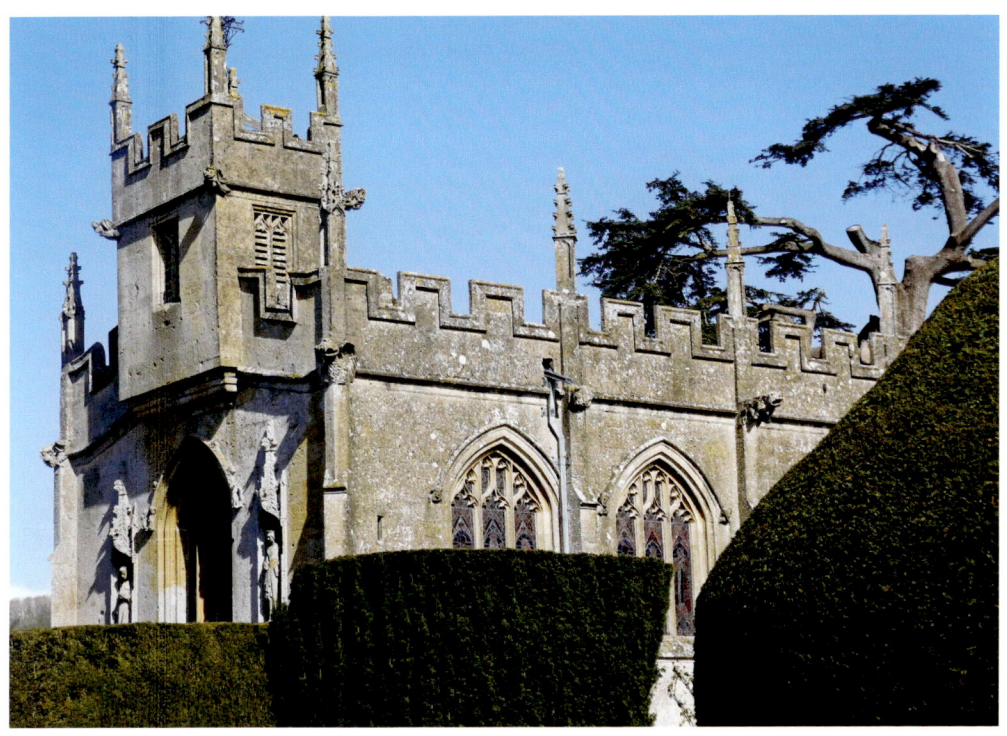

St Mary's Church, Sudeley Castle. (Courtesy of Jamie Robinson)

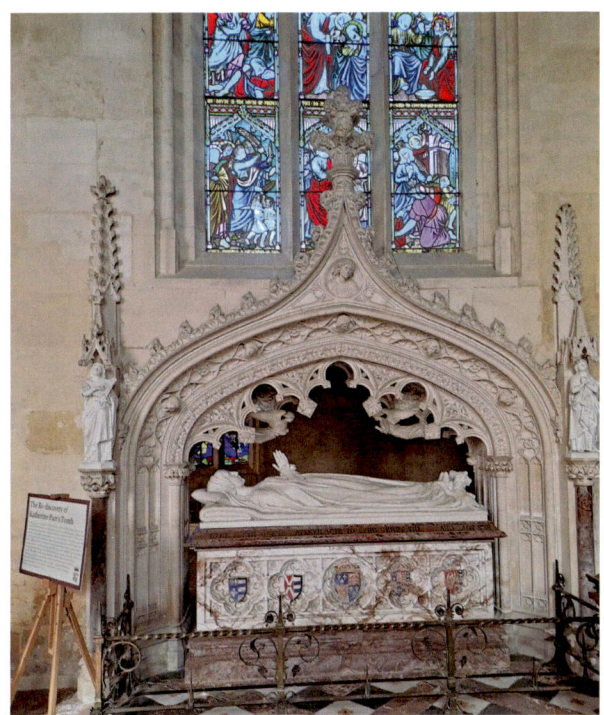

White effigy on the Victorian tomb for Queen Katherine Parr, St Mary's Church, Sudeley Castle.

3

Tewkesbury

By my troth, your town is troubled with
Unruly boys

Comedy of Errors, Act 3, Scene 1

Tewkesbury is sited at the confluence of two great rivers: the Avon and the Severn. The water meadow to the south of the town was the location for the 1471 battle which ended all the hopes of the Lancastrian side in the Wars of the Roses; and from that battle stem many of the eerie tales that haunt Tewkesbury including the magnificent abbey.

Queen Margaret of Anjou's army met the forces of Edward IV in the area known as the Bloody Meadow, where some report hearing the sounds of battle even today. That day her seventeen-year-old son, Edward of Westminster, met his fate, and thus ended any chance of securing the throne for him and for the Lancastrian king, her husband Henry VI. Young Edward's grave takes pride of place in the middle of the monastic choir of the abbey.

Tewkesbury Abbey

This noble building rises above the town, appearing to occupy its own island when Tewkesbury floods – something that happens when the rivers Avon and Swilgate burst their banks. Since the date of the 1471 battle the abbey has been associated with curious tales, along with its role of lifting human hearts to heavenly realms. The official Tewkesbury Abbey handbook puts it like this:

> After a hard and bloody struggle, the Lancastrians were forced to retreat towards the town. Many sought shelter in the Abbey. Some say the Yorkists pursued them inside with unsheathed swords.
>
> Abbot Strensham was celebrating Mass at the high altar. Walking the length of the church holding the Blessed Sacrament, he challenged Edward and his brothers, demanding that the troops should not defile the church with slaughter. The king withdrew, but the Abbot lost an argument about the Abbey's freedom to grant Sanctuary and the Lancastrians were handed over to Edward.

Other accounts suggest that the Lancastrian knights and nobles were dragged out of the abbey two days after first seeking sanctuary there and ordered to be put to death

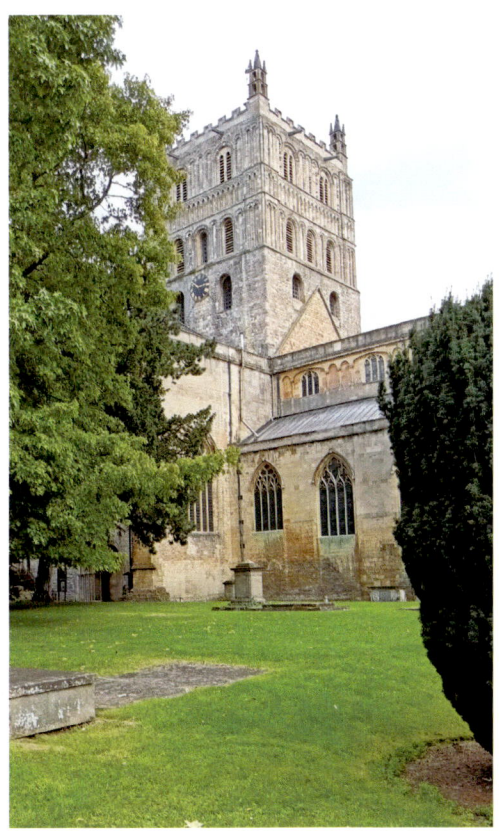

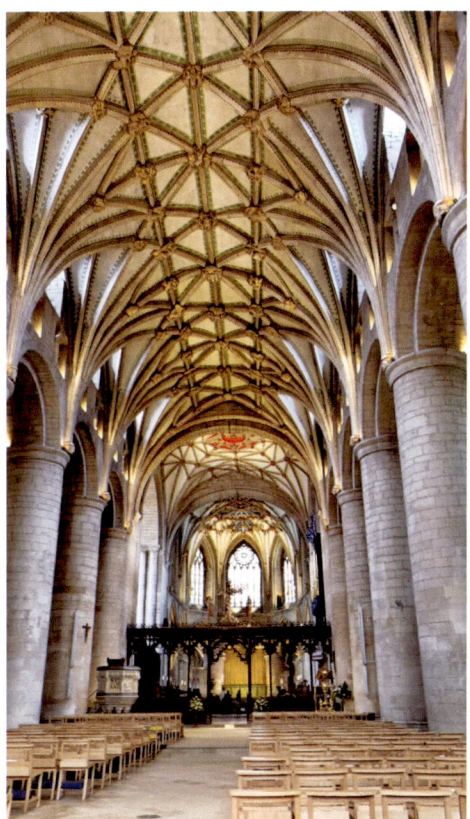

Above left: Tewkesbury Abbey exterior.

Above right: Tewkesbury Abbey interior.

following perfunctory trials. They were beheaded at a scaffold in Church Street during a show trial held at the Cross. Prince Edward was killed in the battle, and his burial in the abbey is marked by a brass plaque in the quire. Uncanny experiences reported in later centuries within the abbey include the sound of moans and screams; it is suggested that these came from the defeated Lancastrians who were ultimately shown no mercy by the victors. The abbey had to be reconsecrated a month after the battle following the violence done within its precincts.

> After the battle, the monks of Tewkesbury are supposed to have picked up pieces of horse armour from the battlefield which they hammered flat to strengthen the door of the sacristy.

Paul reports that in July 2002 he saw a monk in broad daylight gliding up the garden path of the group of ancient cottages just behind the abbey in the cathedral precinct. The monk vanished through the back door of the neighbouring cottage, and Paul thought the apparition had come from the abbey, 'which can be seen from the back gardens of these ancient cottages'.

The Royal Hop Pole

Several historical pubs in Tewkesbury claim to be frequented by the phantoms of soldiers who served either in the Wars of the Roses or in the English Civil War – and in one case, even one from ancient Rome.

The Royal Hop Pole is now a chain-owned pub and restaurant which is situated at 94 Church Street. The building dates back to medieval times and was at one time two separate buildings: a private residence and a coaching inn. On the first floor, staff testify that one area becomes extremely chilly, and they are reluctant to go up there late at night. A night porter reports that he saw Roman soldiers marching in unison across the first-floor landing but only saw them from the waist up. Visitors, too, confirm this sense of unease, and out in the yard one claims to have seen the apparition of a Civil War soldier.

Around the 1950s a staff member went to fill the coal buckets in the yard when he looked up and saw a man staring at him. This silent man was wearing a cloak and riding boots, very much in the style of the Civil War. When the staff member spoke to him, he disappeared.

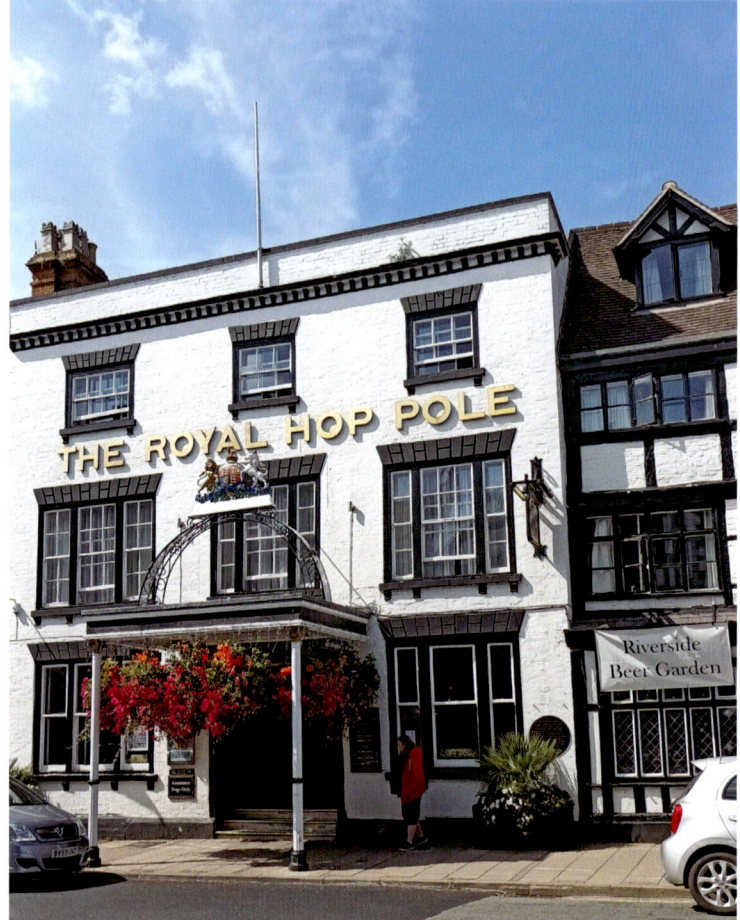

The Royal Hop Pole, Tewkesbury.

The Bell Hotel, Church Street

The half-timbered triple-gabled Bell Hotel is located directly opposite the Gage Gates of the abbey. The date 1696 is inscribed over the front door of the hotel, which has in the past been haunted by the ghost of an elderly gentleman in a top hat and coaching coat. He was regularly seen in the lounge bar sitting at a table awaiting service, but when asked by the staff what he would like to order he mysteriously disappeared.

The Bell Hotel was originally known as the Angel and may have briefly been known as the Ring of Bells in 1800. Later, it became the Bell and Bowling Green Hotel. On one of the interior walls of the former bar there was a large carving of the royal arms of William of Orange; this disappeared when the wall was removed to incorporate the bar into a new dining area. During these changes, another feature of the inn disappeared: an old portrait which formerly hung on the wall depicting a gentleman with the same characteristics as the reported phantom. It is said that he has not been seen since the painting was removed.

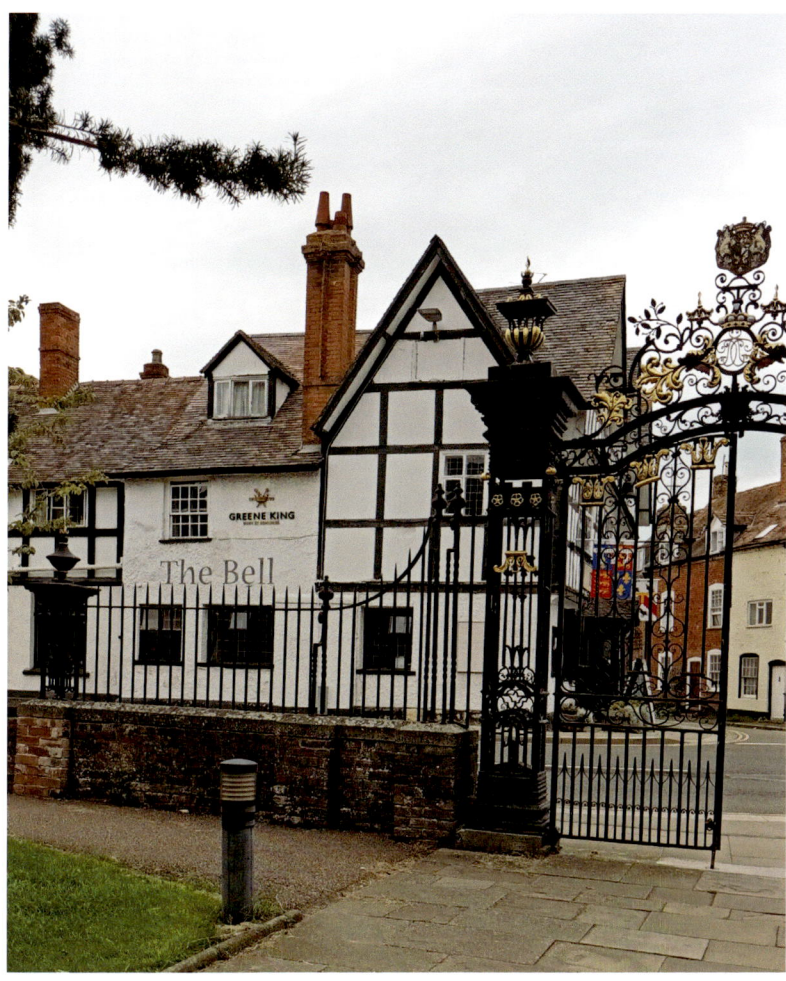

The Bell, Tewkesbury.

Ye Olde Black Bear

Ye Olde Black Bear was established in 1308 and is claimed to be the oldest pub in Gloucestershire that has always been a pub. It is reputedly haunted by several apparitions. Most documented is the little old lady dressed in black who used to sit in a corner of the snug bar. Customers have been known to order a drink for her only to find she had mysteriously disappeared. Poltergeist activity has been reported too: a set of horseshoes that used to hang on the wall in the former restaurant was seen to fly off the wall, ending up several yards across the room without any apparent logical explanation.

The pub was closed for refurbishment for several years and reopened in June 2023. Amongst its unique features is as leather ceiling in one of the bars and a glass-covered stairwell whose stairs lead to a secret passageway that monks used five centuries ago to get to the abbey.

Among the apparitions glimpsed in certain rooms and corridors of Ye Olde Black Bear, we may number a cavalier and a chain-dragging headless man. Writer Michele Eve speculates that this headless man may have been a Lancastrian soldier who was executed further up from the Black Bear. The vengeful Yorkist victors of the Battle of Tewkesbury would have hunted down and killed any surviving enemy warriors. As previously mentioned, knights and nobles took shelter in the abbey, vainly hoping they could claim sanctuary. Many common Lancastrian soldiers who'd escaped the carnage met their deaths in other ways; drowned in the River Swilgate or the River Avon or captured and executed. Certainly, Ye Olde Black Bear would have been one of the places to which Lancastrian soldiers may have fled, and few would have survived. Some present-day visitors believe that the spirit of one decapitated soldier fled to Ye Olde Black Bear with his comrades not realising he was dead and has stayed there ever since.

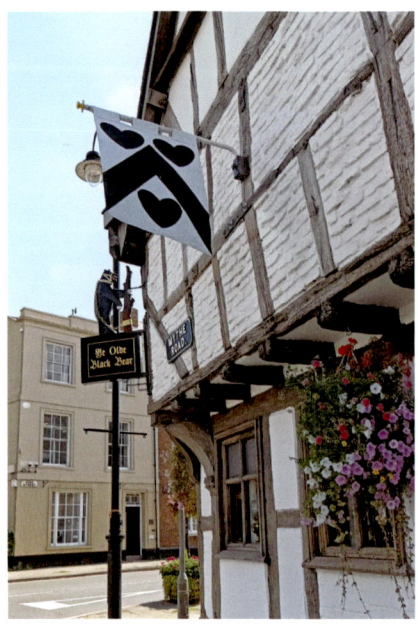

Ye Olde Black Bear, Tewkesbury.

Tolsey Lane

Tolsey Lane adjoins the High Street at the business premises of a firm of funeral directors. On the opposite corner, a substantial merchant's house known as Cross House occupies the site of the medieval Courthouse of the Lords of Tewkesbury. This property has undergone a full Victorian-style restoration and for the past few years has been the Cross House Tavern.

Tolsey Lane is one of the oldest roads in Tewkesbury, and one of the strange events reported here is a ghostly Victorian funeral procession that passes along the lane at night, led by undertakers and pallbearers all wearing full black mourning garb including top hats with veils, along with a coffin in a horse-drawn hearse. This sight has been reported by many, even police officers.

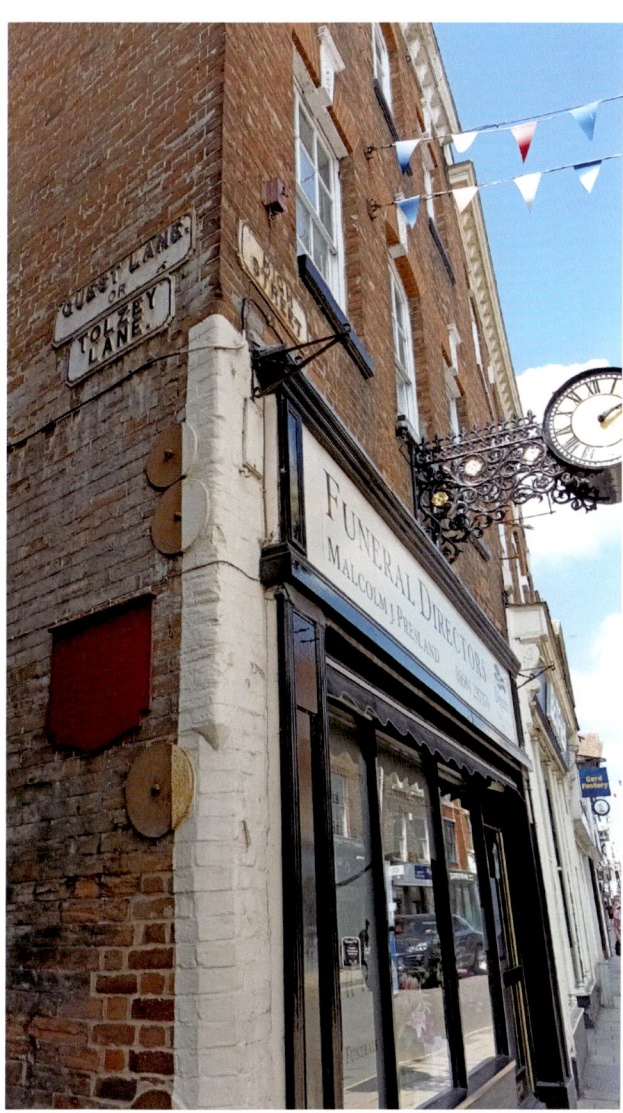

Tolsey Lane, Tewkesbury.

4

Tetbury and Surrounds

> The bloody parliament shall this be called
>
> *Henry VI Part III,* Act 1, Scene 1

Chavenage House, near Tetbury

The gracious house at Chavenage mostly dates from 1576, when it replaced the medieval manor house that preceded it, on monastic land confiscated from the Church by Henry VIII. The successful wool-farming Fitz Stephen family were delighted to snap up that land after the dissolution of the Monasteries: a prime location at the top of a hill, ideal for them as a rich family to showcase their status. They changed their name to Stephens, and the property's owner became Edward Stephens. Many uncanny tales emanate from this property; the most famous, 'The Curse of Chavenage', relates to the Rump Parliament of Oliver Cromwell and the intense pressure Parliament exerted on MPs to sign a death warrant for King Charles I.

The Lowsley-Williams family are the present owners of Chavenage with George Lowsley-Williams and his two sisters Caroline Lowsley-Williams and Joanna Gouriet

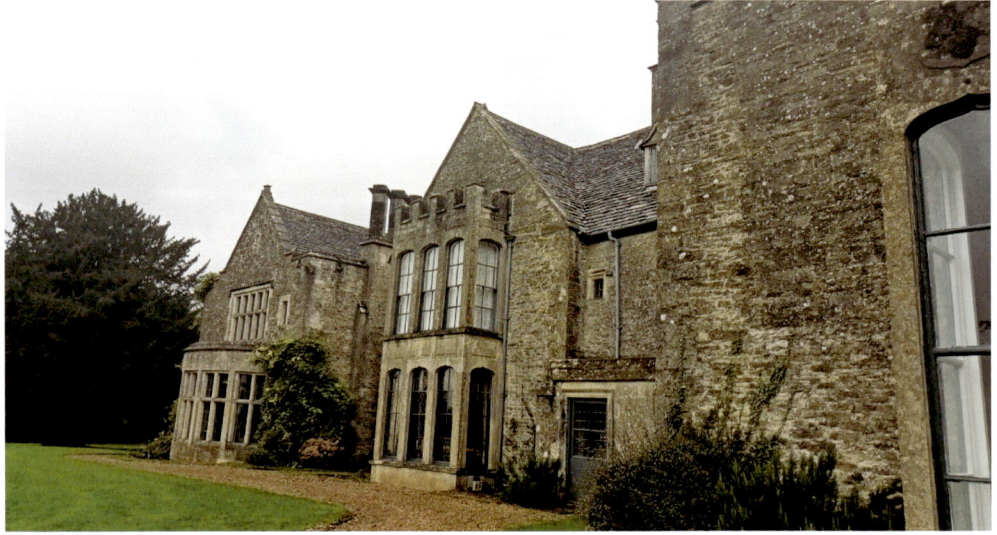

Back of Chavenage House.

being the current custodians. George, the eldest sibling, describes the events which led to the Chavenage Curse. In 1658 the Civil War had ended, and Charles I was imprisoned in Carisbrooke Castle in the Isle of Wight. 'Oliver Cromwell had a bit of a problem: what was he going to do with the King? To end the war forever, he had to get rid of the king. Unfortunately for Charles, it was a bit terminal.'

So, Cromwell decided he would have to go round England and personally canvas prominent MPs to vote for the king's execution. The owner of Chavenage at that time was Nathaniel Stephens, the influential MP for Gloucestershire. Colonel Stephens had driven off a Royalist siege and saved Gloucester for the Parliamentarians. He was an important well-known local figure and a war hero; if he voted a certain way, others would follow. Nathaniel, however, was not keen on the idea of the king's execution. Cromwell visited Chavenage, stayed in the room now known as Cromwell's Room, and although he kept Nathaniel up all night talking, Nathaniel flatly refused to sign the king's death warrant. Cromwell left Chavenage frustrated with his mission unfulfilled, only to return a month later, by which time Nathaniel had become very ill. George relates the story:

> He caved in to get rid of Cromwell. 'Oh all right I'll vote with you.' Abigail, his daughter, was so appalled when she heard he was going to vote for the king's execution that she stormed into his sickroom and laid a curse on him and all future lords of the manor. He was now dying. When all the family and friends were gathered here to witness the death of the old Colonel, they realised that a carriage had come in through the main gates that was even more embellished than any of the others present. It stopped at the front door whereupon the old man died; his shroud was seen to rise from his body, drift through the house, enter the coach which then drove off, but not so quickly that the bystanders couldn't see that the coachman was a beheaded man still wearing the royal vestments; and on his knee was the royal garter; and as it went out through the gate it was seen to be devoured by the flames of hell.

The legend continues that ever since, until the Stephens line became extinct, whenever the lord of the manor died, the same ghost of the king appeared to carry him off. Abigail had laid an effective curse on the man who gave in to the will of what might well be known to history as 'the bloody parliament'.

'That was the start of our ghost stories,' says George, who gave us a tour of the house, beginning with Cromwell's Room, renowned for the magnificent Mortlake tapestries which line the walls and depict an idealised view of 'the New World'. George says:

> I did take a Halloween group round at night; as you've noticed, there's no electricity in this room, so you have to carry a candle. All the shutters were shut; suddenly a gust of breeze from somewhere blew most of the candles out – that was quite spooky, we were standing there, all the candles went out, it was pitch dark, closest I came to feeling there was a ghost in this room.

Following the purchase of the estate by Edward Stephens, it has only been in the hands of two families: the Stephens and now the Lowsley-Williams. The latter family have owned Chavenage since 1891, when it was purchased by the present owners'

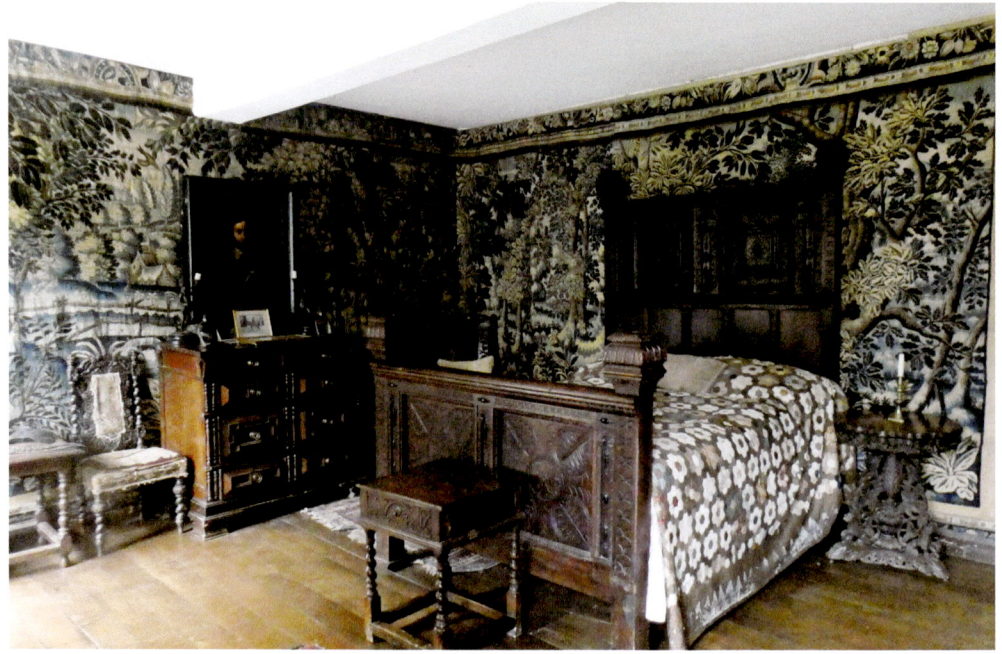

Cromwell's Room, Chavenage House. (Courtesy of Jamie Robinson)

great-grandfather. George, Caroline and Joanna took custodianship of the property after the death of their father David at the age of eighty-nine in April 2023.

During his life there, David (1933–2023) was equally intrigued by the uncanny events at Chavenage. On one occasion he was sitting in the great hall by the fire reading the newspaper and became aware that the dogs had tensed; they looked up and growled. He watched the two of them turning their heads together and following the progress of something invisible from the main door across the hall. David tried to rationalise it by telling himself they must have detected a rat running below, under the floorboards. Caroline says: 'The dogs occasionally growl at something that's not seen…But basically I think they're friendly ghosts, I've not had any trouble … This was all we knew as our childhood playground.'

David's favourite unworldly visitor, George tells us, was probably the monk. A young army padre who had been asked to lead a service in the chapel mentioned seeing the monk sitting with his head down and had wanted to go and ask him how long he planned to stay but felt he couldn't as the monk was so deep in prayer. Visitors report that after entering the chapel the monk joins them but then he disappears. Others see the monk as they approach the chapel; one of these was a very down-to-earth Australian tourist.

The great hall was a favourite location for interior scenes in the TV series *Poldark*. The family are shown eating at the long table in the hall when Ross Poldark first reappears having unexpectedly returned from the American Civil War to discover the unwelcome changes that have taken place since his departure. An outstanding feature of this hall is the magnificent stained glass. George noted that when the Stephens family were wanting to embellish their house, 'if you wanted to save yourself a bit of

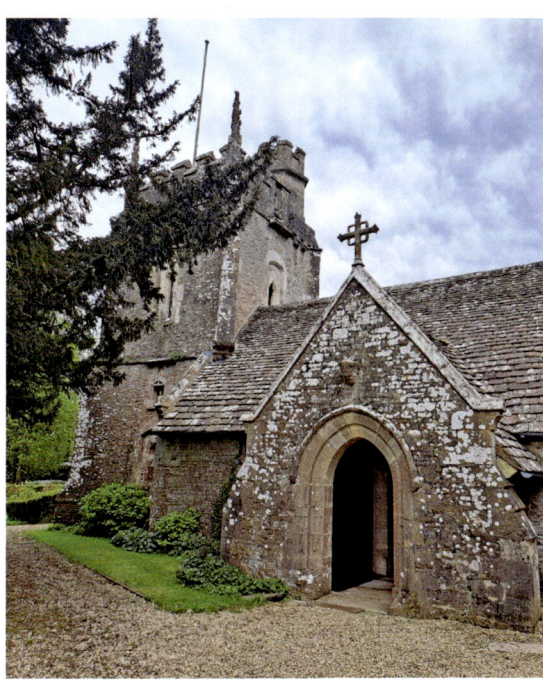

South door of the chapel,
Chavenage House.

money you went and took what you wanted from the monastery'. Accordingly, the house contains several items removed from the monastery building and brought here.

George's childhood bedroom in the Victorian extension sounds as if it wasn't the ideal location for a peaceful night: 'Unfortunately, the room that I was put in had to be exorcised twice by my great- grandmother. Originally my room was a guest room and the guests complained that in the middle of the night a spooky figure would be leaning over them, with heavy epaulettes on his shoulder.'

Several independently mentioned that this uninvited visitor had long dark greasy hair, a 'Mexican style' moustache, and gold epaulettes. Beatrice Mary, his great-grandmother, got the local Anglican vicar in to do an exorcism; but nothing seemed to work, so she decided to cover all options and got a Roman Catholic priest in as well. That didn't work either; the disturbing vision kept appearing, so they abandoned the room. George goes on to say that when his parents David and Rona took over the house and estate, they decided this was a waste of a room, so 'they painted it with a nice jolly colour,' put young George in that room, and he grew up with this room as his bedroom.

> I do remember every night I could only go to sleep with my head well under the pillows because I didn't want to see what was happening around the room. I could hear things, I could feel things, but I never actually saw anything, and I wouldn't come out from under the pillow till I could hear the birds singing in the morning when I knew it was light, and was then safe, and I could come out.

On one occasion Caroline's friend Charles stayed in the room, which came to be known as room number one, and he told her later he had been terrified, as he'd felt as if his blankets were suddenly made of lead and pressing down on him, and he couldn't get up whichever way he moved. When Charles at last managed to get up he went to the door, found himself locked in and was about to scream, when better counsel prevailed and he decided to go back to bed, where he lay down and went to sleep. In the morning all seemed perfectly normal. Caroline adds: 'No-one's slept in there since … It is a funny room. Paranormal Site Investigators came to the house and when they pointed their "ghoul meters" at number one, their meters went off the scale. So that's possibly the most haunted room in the house.'

George also describes his sighting of a ghost when he was very young and camping with his schoolfriend on the lawn, about 20 metres from the house. They both woke up at about 4 a.m. and peered out of the tent into the misty morning and saw the dark image of a man on horseback, wearing a wide hat. They shot back inside the tent and zipped themselves in tight to their sleeping bags and were so frightened they had to wait for someone to come and find them rather than venture out of the tent again. 'It was a very strange experience looking out from our little tent and seeing this figure on his horse. Both of us today over fifty years later still remember looking out of our tiny tent, seeing that spooky horse-rider over the other side of the lawn.'

Another phantom is known as the White Lady. She has been seen several times, mainly out on the lawn leading to the fields between Chavenage and Beverston Castle.

Beverston Castle is a Norman stronghold about a mile away from Chavenage, which could formerly be seen at the end of the west vista from the lawn at the back of the house. Shakespeare describes the district of Beverston in his play *Richard III* – his and the Hathaway families were associated with this area and are mentioned in the parish registers of St Mary's Church, Beverston, which go back to 1565. That castle view is now obscured by trees. One Trip Adviser reviewer said: 'It is such a romantic and historic place, it is just lovely to wander alone, and appreciate the very special atmosphere.' It had a very different atmosphere during the Civil War when it was a Royalist castle.

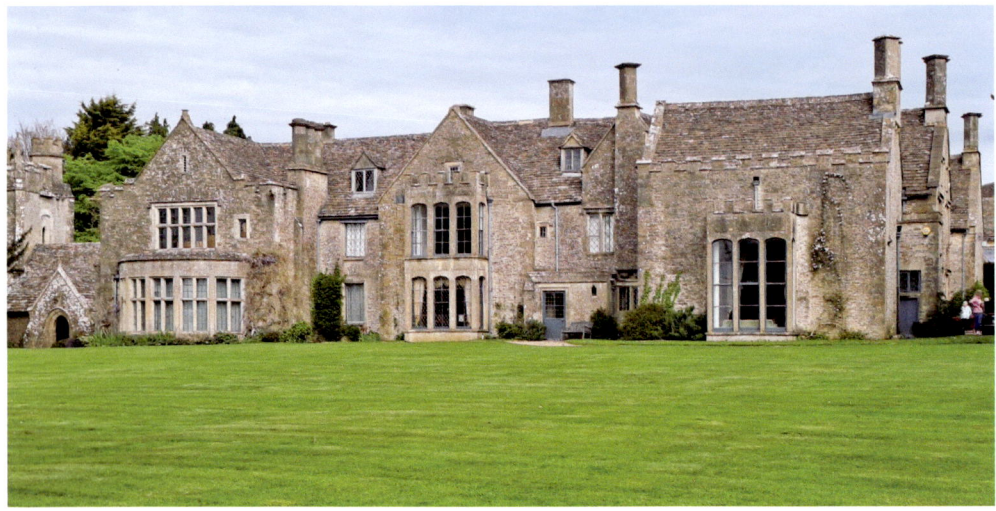

The lawn at the back of Chavenage House where the two schoolboys George Lowsley-Williams and his friend camped.

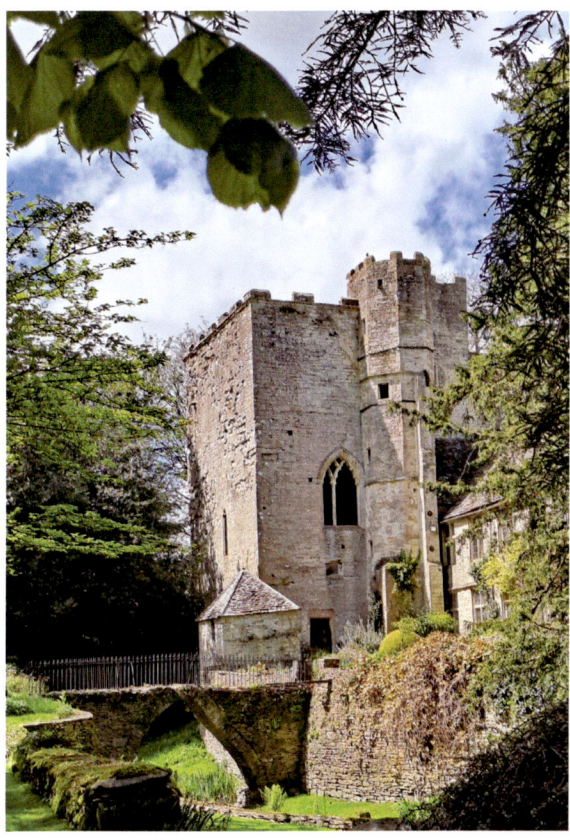

Beverston Castle.

'We were Parliamentarians here,' says George, 'and for four years we besieged the castle from this house but could never get in.'

However, there was a young lady at Chavenage, and her boyfriend was the major at Beverston. 'To meet him she'd signal from the tiny little window directly pointing toward the castle; she'd light a lantern and put it in that window'.

It was agreed between them the signal meant no Parliamentary attack was planned that night. Major Ogglethorpe would see the light in the tiny ground-floor window from Beverston, leave his post, and come and visit her in the fields. As a consequence, Beverston always knew when an attack was planned from Chavenage, and all attacks so far had failed. But the Roundheads at Chavenage started to get suspicious and discovered what was going on. They set an ambush and as Ogglethorpe approached Chavenage the major was set upon, and according to Caroline: '…beaten up and dragged back to Beverston and then hanged from his own ramparts, parts of his body scattered around. His girlfriend found out what had happened and, so upset at her part in his demise, she took her own life.'

George adds, 'One of our ghost stories says that if you see a light shining through that window her spirit is abroad'. Now, dressed in white and holding a lit candle, she wanders between Chavenage and Beverston trying to warn her beloved not to come out. Several sightings of the White Lady have been reported. Caroline concludes: 'The ghosts are part of our family, if that's the right expression.'

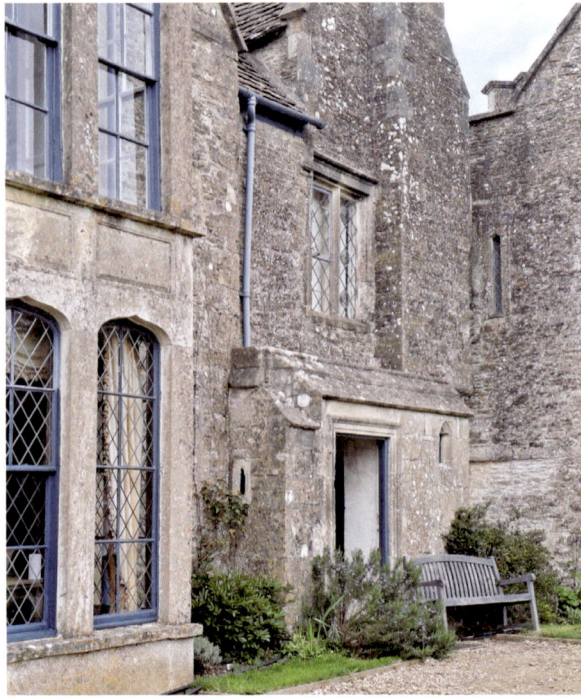

Tiny window exterior,
Chavenage House.

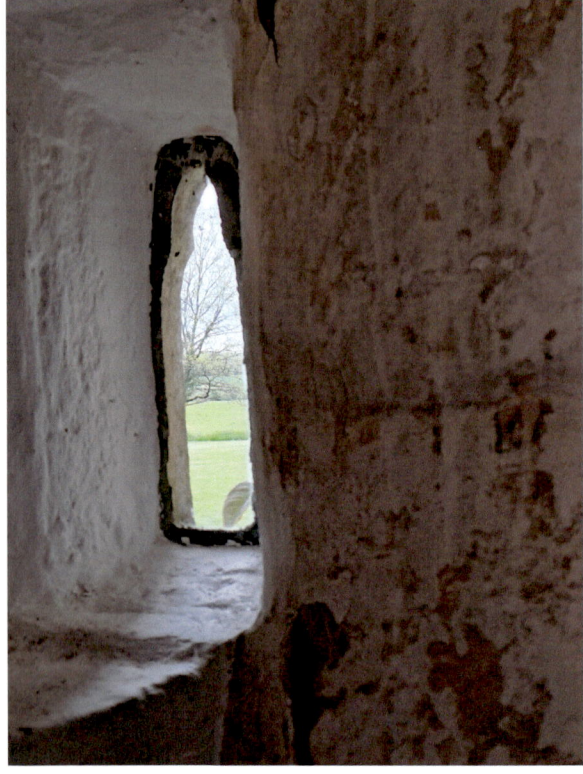

Tiny window interior,
Chavenage House.

5

Wotton-under-Edge

O monstrous! O strange! We are haunted.

A Midsummer Night's Dream, Act 3, Scene 1

The Ancient Ram Inn

This richly atmospheric property was first built in the year 1145 to provide a church house for the local village priest to live in. It is sited over a pagan burial ground on the main road through Wotton-under-Edge. John Humphries purchased the Ancient Ram in 1968 from Whitbread's Brewery, and then began a period of restoration, dedicated to preserving this historic treasure. John's family were initially not so keen on his purchase. Caroline, who has owned the house since the death of her father John at the age of eighty-nine on 12 December 2017, recalls that time. She says:

> My dad bought it, and I was seven when we moved in. I said, 'Daddy what have you done?' There were cockroaches and … He had originally bought it to be a guest house, but customers kept leaving in the middle of the night … Dad suspected it was haunted but it was confirmed by guests. He didn't know it was haunted when he bought it.

Since she inherited the property from her father, she has herself experienced a number of peculiar happenings. 'My dad's picture was flying across the kitchen,' she says.

Undaunted by his family's initial reluctance, from the year 1968, John spent all his spare money and time restoring the Ancient Ram. In his restoration work he uncovered old oak timbers, original stone walls and a rare example of a medieval window. He also followed up every clue about the history of the building and obtained documents from the County Records Office which traced an unbroken line of ownership from 1350 to the time of John's purchase in 1968.

John offered bed and breakfast at the Ancient Ram in the summer months for those who love spending the night in an ancient house with oak beamed ceilings, steep staircases, wide, creaking floorboards – and numerous phantoms. In the oak-timbered rooms where pilgrims and priests had once gathered, John worked hard to keep up an 800-year tradition of hospitality. But he began to get letters from former guests who, knowing nothing of the building's haunted history, detailed some eerie happenings during their stay. John said that some of his guests had booked for three or four nights then left after only one night. 'Others wouldn't even step into the bedroom known

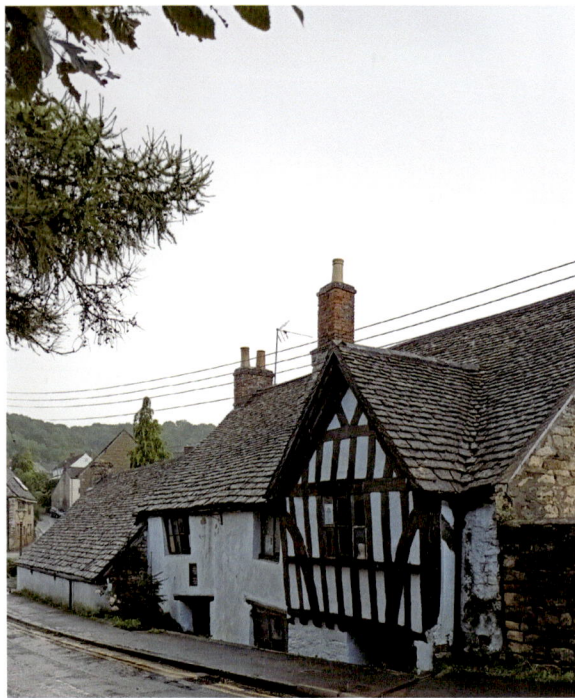

The Ancient Ram,
Wotton-under-Edge.

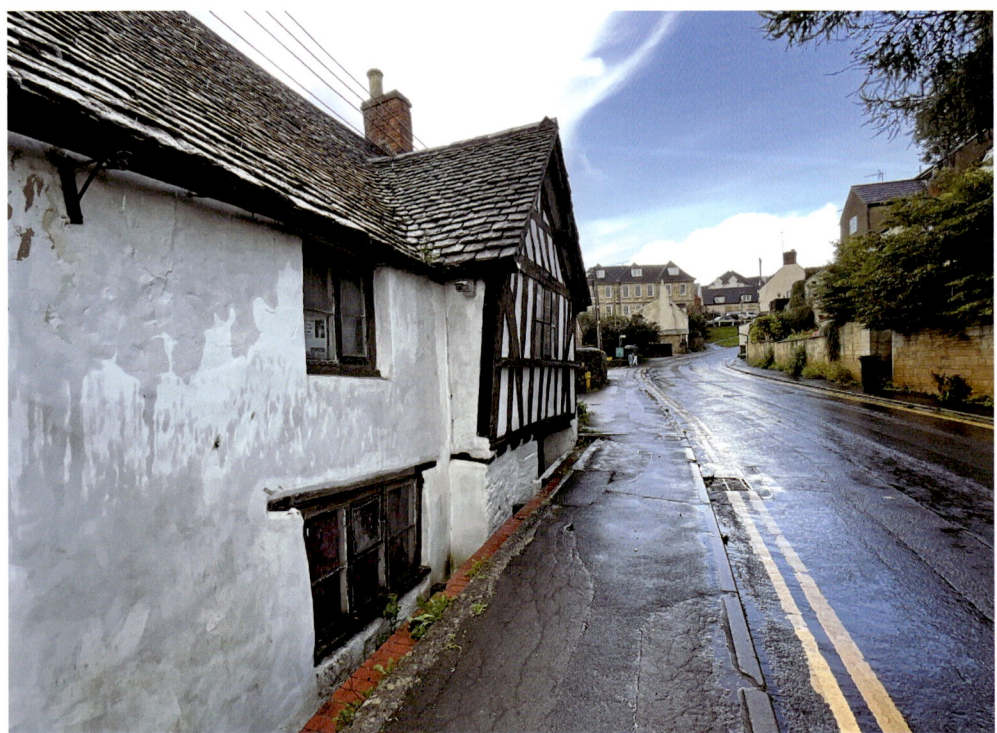

The side of the Ancient Ram, Wotton-under-Edge. (Courtesy of Jamie Robinson)

as "the Bishop's Room" which has the reputation of being the most haunted room in the house.'

A visit to the Ancient Ram today captivates visitors with its rich and distinctive atmosphere, enhanced by the bizarre objects displayed in every room. Among these is a mummified cat discovered in the house during renovations. Now on display in the living room in a glass case, this cat was found by John either behind a fireplace or inside a wall. A notice informs us that Stroud Museum had confirmed it was dead before being placed in the building and could be 400–500 years old. In those times, it was customary to place a cat inside the walls of the home to ward off evil spirits or as a good luck charm. It was believed that cats had a sixth sense and that putting one in the wall was a blood sacrifice so the animal could use psychic abilities to find and ward off unwanted spirits.

As visitors tour the Ancient Ram they encounter a sinister raven with outspread wings suspended from the ceiling; a snarling fox's head on the wall; two rams' heads on the inglenook; and numerous crucifixes and figurines of the Virgin Mary. In the Bishop's Room a black soft toy bear on the red bedcover challenges those who enter, with its disturbing glass eyes. Elsewhere in the house, a skeleton, Egyptian bust, and clown all contribute to the ambiance. In addition, the Christian texts adorning the walls all over the house give the impression that in order to keep his disembodied housemates at bay, John was covering all options. One text states: 'Christ is the silent listener to every conversation in this house.'

During my tour of the house alongside a number of other visitors, I entered the Children's Den, where creepy dolls train their unnerving gaze upon all visitors, especially the one sitting in a child's cot in the righthand corner of the room. One thoroughly spooked visitor said: 'That doll was on the other side of the room a few moments ago and now it's on this side of the room.'

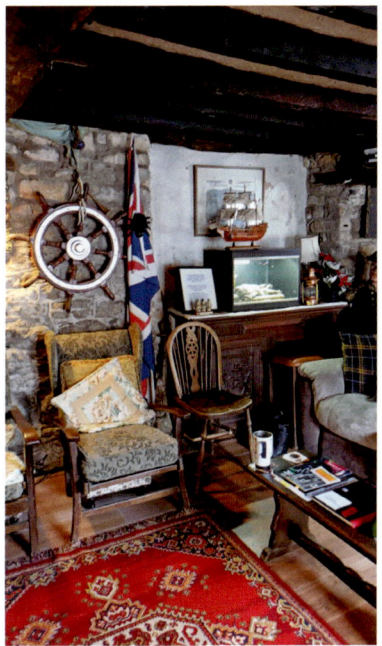

Seating area at the Ancient Ram featuring a mummified cat, Wotton-under-Edge.

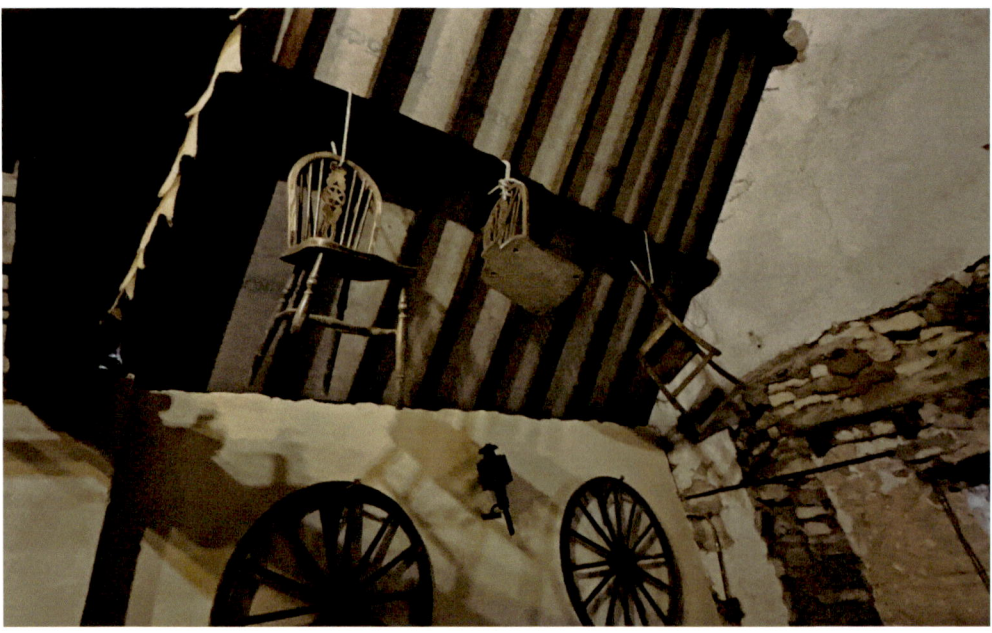

Hanging chairs in the roof of the barn, the Ancient Ram, Wotton-under-Edge. (Courtesy of Jamie Robinson)

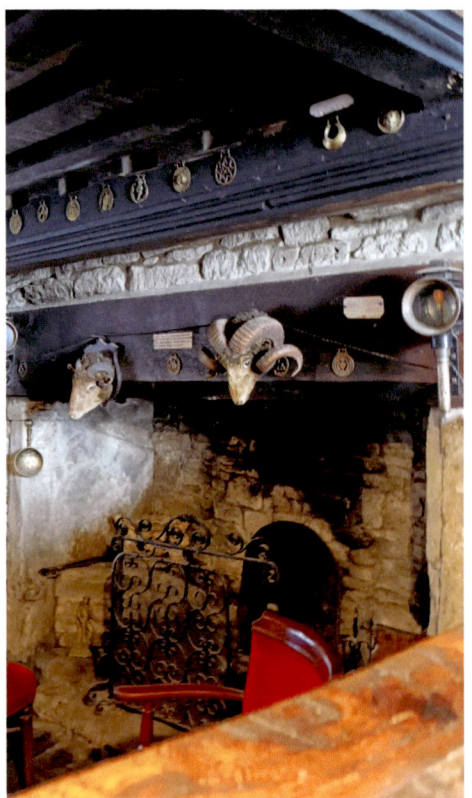

Rams' heads above the inglenook, the Ancient Ram, Wotton-under-Edge.

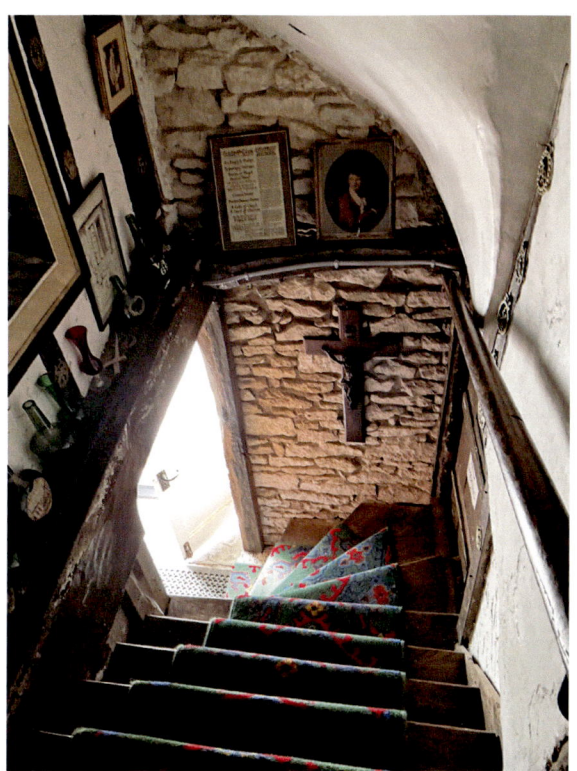

Staircase between ground and first floor of the Ancient Ram, Wotton-under-Edge. (Courtesy of Jamie Robinson)

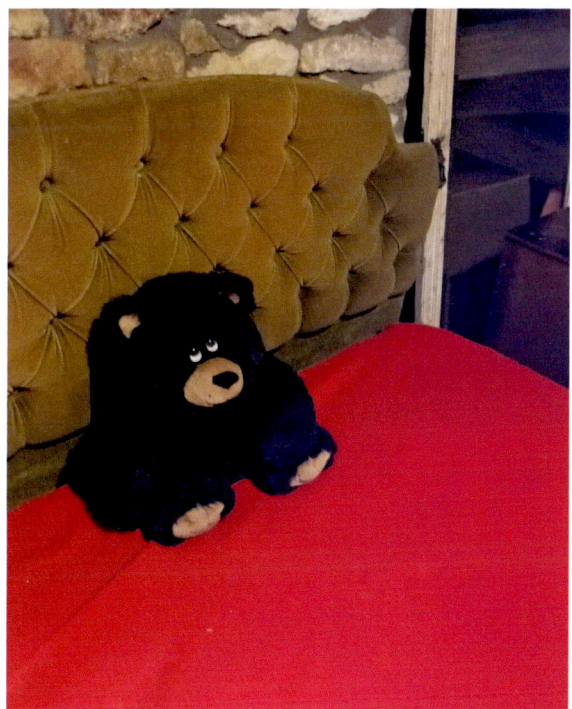

Black soft toy bear on the bed in the Bishop's Room, the Ancient Ram, Wotton-under-Edge.

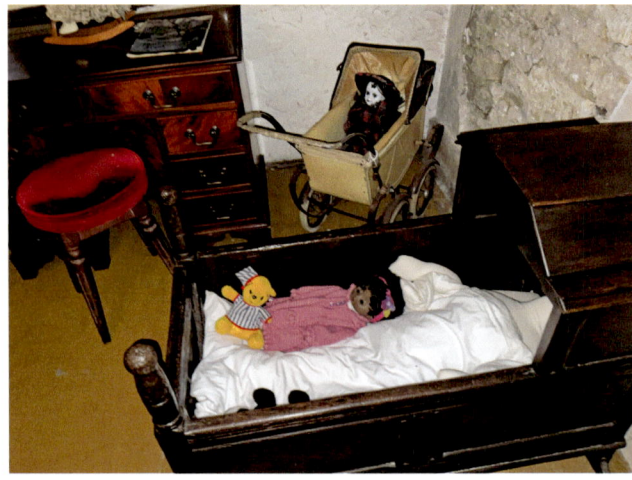

Victorian dolls in the
Children's Den, the Ancient
Ram, Wotton-under-Edge.
(Courtesy of Jamie Robinson)

During his research John discovered that at one time the building housed the carpenters and stonemasons working on Wotton's parish church. From 1145, the property continued in the ownership of the church for 400 years. Pilgrims used to stay there, and it was also a favourite haunt of highwaymen.

John reported seeing a spectral cavalier in full uniform, while guests claimed to have witnessed figures walking through walls. Sightings reported over the years have included, in addition to the cavalier, a monk, a young woman called Elizabeth who walks around with a candle in her hand, and a character known locally as Old Tom the Ostler. John later learned that a cavalier had been killed in the house and young Elizabeth, too, had been murdered. It is believed that Elizabeth's body lay beneath the former bar in a blocked-up cellar. John had also mentioned a tunnel leading from the pub towards the church about 200 yards away.

Now, at the time of writing, Caroline plans to carry out all the current improvement work needed and then to use the property for community events, wedding ceremonies, regular open days, and possibly a restaurant. She would also like to host schoolchildren for living history lessons. In addition, she takes film crews, and this income helps her maintain the property.

Visitors have offered some of the following accounts: Jason confirms that during his 1999 visit, upon entry to the Weaver's Attic, he heard the faint sound of a young girl crying. Jo Cook reports that as she explored the building one night with friends she saw 'dancing lights', felt a drop in temperature, and discerned shadowy faces. Melanie Newman recalls her experience here at the age of fifteen, when she saw 'the grey lady'. Not everyone feels fearful in the Ancient Ram, though. Another visitor, Phillip, maintains that he was perfectly comfortable with the atmosphere. 'The spirits don't harm me. I feel safe there. I spent hours in the Bishop's Room by myself and I loved it. I have been twice and want to go again.'

I agree, from personal experience, with Phillip, but would feel nervous at the prospect of spending the night in any room there, especially alone. In particular, the bedroom in the roof did have a rather creepy feeling. In that room one may hear an uncanny low roar – but it is probably the sound of vehicles moving past in the road outside. It still remains a rather odd sound for passing traffic to make.

6

Arlingham

Where souls do couch on flowers we'll hand in hand,
And with our sprightly port make the ghosts gaze

Anthony and Cleopatra, Act 4, Scene 14

Within the Horseshoe Loop of the River Severn may be found the ancient village of Arlingham. Much busier and more accessible at the time of the Roman occupation, this quiet little community offers the perfect setting for those seeking rural tranquillity – and also for ghosts to linger.

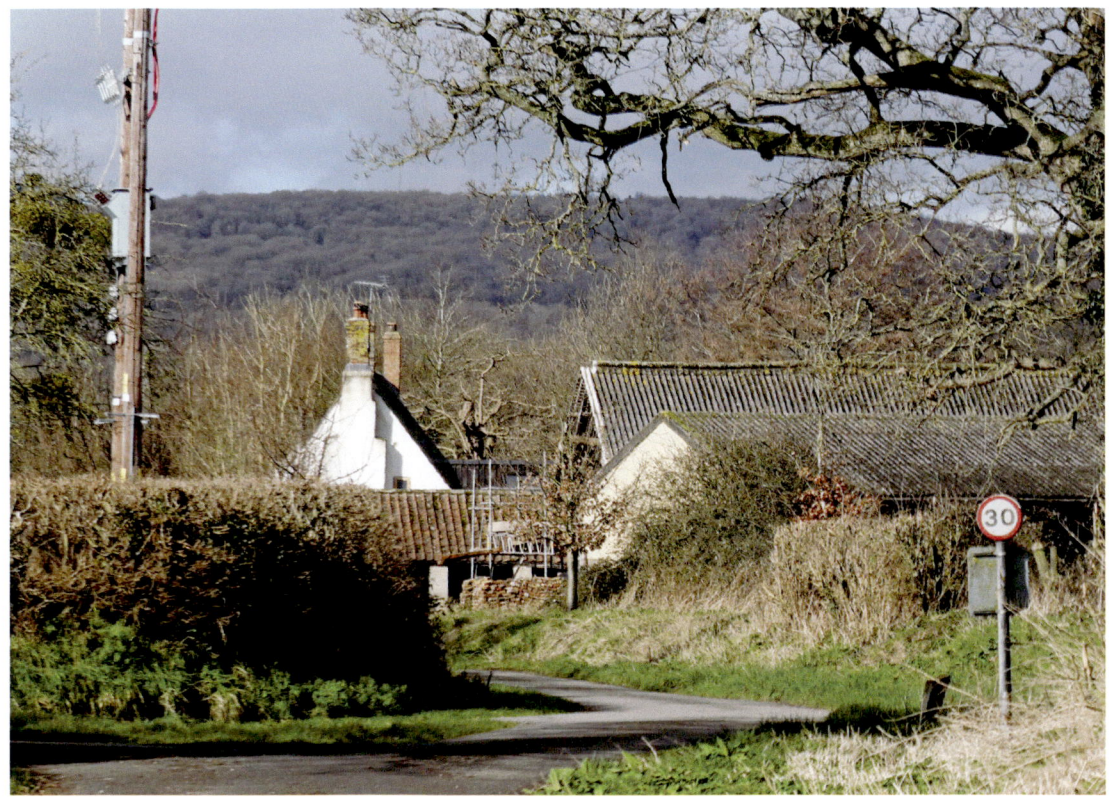

Arlingham village. (Courtesy of Jamie Robinson)

Slowwe House, Silver Street

This was certainly the case for the hippie community who in the 1960s chose the tumbledown property Slowwe House for their new home. They considered it an ideal location for their new life of freedom, co-operation and self-sufficiency; but having moved into the dilapidated front wing, they began to experience strange things. It is said that they were so disturbed by what they felt and saw in the place, the commune members called in a priest to perform an exorcism.

The house was originally called 'Slo' or 'Sloo' House. Much of the house as we see it today probably originates from the fifteenth century, but the Domesday Book includes a listing of the house which was occupied at that time. The site is known to have been used during Roman times; the courtyard is considered to be from that period, and a Roman coffin was discovered in the present garden area. Arlingham has a large number of notable old properties. It is quite possible that dwellings have existed on or near the present site for thousands of years possibly as far back as the Stone Age, as evidence of Bronze Age and Iron Age settlers has been found in the area.

Slowwe House continued to appeal to non-establishment figures. During the 1970s a progressive rock band called Paladin lived and rehearsed in Slowwe House where they would invite people from the music industry to listen to their music. There is no record of either band members or visitors having experienced anything unearthly, so it seems the priest the hippies called in did a good job; but that was only the front wing of the house. Perhaps it hadn't occurred to them that the back wing (the east wing) may have needed some spiritual attention too. Members of the Lacey family confirmed this when, in the same decade, they purchased that wing; it wasn't long before they began to witness apparitions of 'The Grey Lady'.

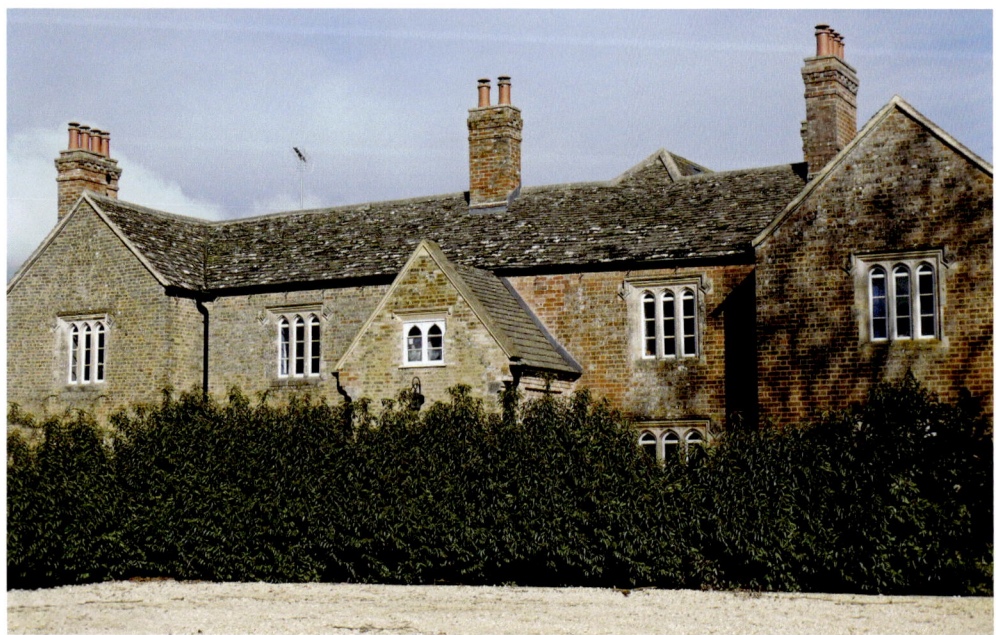

Slowwe House, Arlingham. (Courtesy of Jamie Robinson)

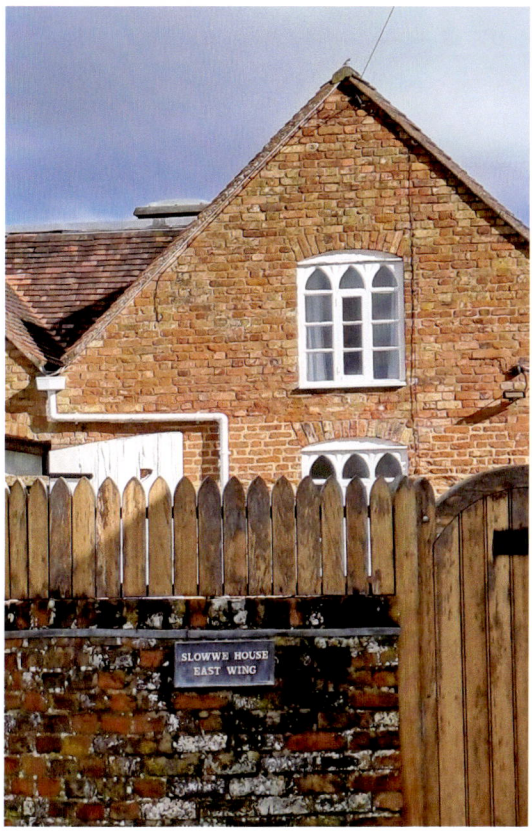

East wing of Slowwe House, Arlingham.

The family moved into the barn so they could gut the building as it was in a dire state. When they started the renovations, the disquieting activity began; lights kept being switched on in the house, even though they had ensured all lights were turned off. So, they would often need to return to the house to switch the lights off – on one evening they returned three times. Windows would open and shut by themselves when no one was in the house. As the building work ended, they started to decorate the walls with their favourite pictures, but these pictures kept falling off. In particular, one picture was taken off the wall so often so that Mrs Lacey never bothered putting that picture back up again.

Mrs Lacey maintained that the family didn't take too much notice of these happenings until one day when she looked out through a window and saw a ghostly female form crossing the courtyard. This lady wore a long grey dress and a grey bonnet; when Mrs Lacey looked away for a few moments, then turned back, the figure had disappeared. Later, Mrs Lacey saw the grey lady again this time inside the house. Whilst in the kitchen she turned round to get something from the worktop and observed the grey lady right behind her who then disappeared in front of her eyes. The apparition was also spotted walking along the landing and then vanishing. It seemed she liked the guest bedroom as she was often seen there by the family and their guests. The two young daughters of the Lacey family occasionally slept in that room and reported the presence of the grey lady standing in the room when they awoke.

Court House

The manor house at Arlingham Court, substantially rebuilt in the mid-fifteenth century, was occupied for over 300 years, but by 1882 Arlingham Court, empty for the past few decades and in ruins, was demolished. A property remained, known as Court House, and it formed the scene for an uncanny case of foretelling of a future event. On 24 May 1757 the residents, the Yate family, saw a shadowy funeral procession make its way up the avenue to Court House. In 1758, John Yate, the last Yate family heir died. It was exactly a year from the date of that strange foretelling. Subsequently ownership passed on, and the house has followed the fate of Arlingham Court.

Across the river at the top of the Horseshoe may be found Newnham-on-Severn, a busy port in Roman times; there, three important roads converged, including the major military coast road, and a ford existed linking the Forest of Dean with the Roman road network at Arlingham. This ford was still passable until around 1802 when the river changed channel, shifted and took away the sand bank that gave access to the fordable, though dangerous, rocky causeway. After that a ferry carried passengers across the river; at Newnham the present White Hart Inn was formerly the Passage House, a coaching inn for travellers planning to cross the river to Arlingham where they would find the busy Passage Inn – now sadly derelict, having followed the fate of many old pubs in our times of economic crisis. The Passage Inn (at the time of writing) sits sadly waiting at Arlingham, creating a feeling of loneliness and desolation, awaiting full renovation and a return to life; while the White Hart thrives at Newnham, a popular and lively destination, especially for those gathering to see the Severn Bore.

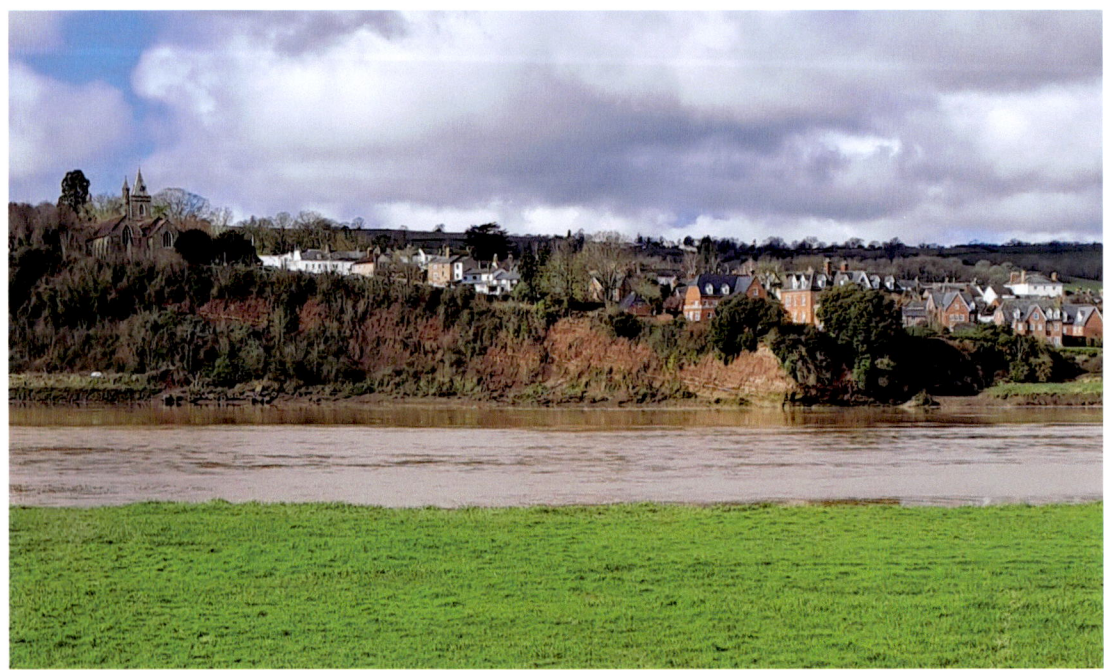

View from Arlingham to St Peter's Church, Newnham, across the top of the Severn Horseshoe.

7

Cirencester

Why all these gliding ghosts

Julius Caesar, Act 1, Scene 3

The town of Cirencester also has a history going back to the Roman occupation and may lay claim to many curious paranormal events. Several of these have been reported inside the local hostelries, of which the following two establishments are a representative pair.

The King's Head Hotel

The hotel, standing in the marketplace opposite the parish church, has a reputation of being one of the most haunted places in Cirencester. Some of its architectural features date back to the fourteenth century. I have visited the hotel myself on more than one occasion and have felt a curious atmosphere there, which persists both on the ground floor and the stairs to the vaulted cellar. A vision of a monk with no face reportedly scared one member of staff into quitting her job. Guests have also reported paranormal activity, such as their room doors opening, and the ghostly image of an armoured man walking through the ballroom. Several phantoms have been spotted, including an English Civil War Cavalier and a monk.

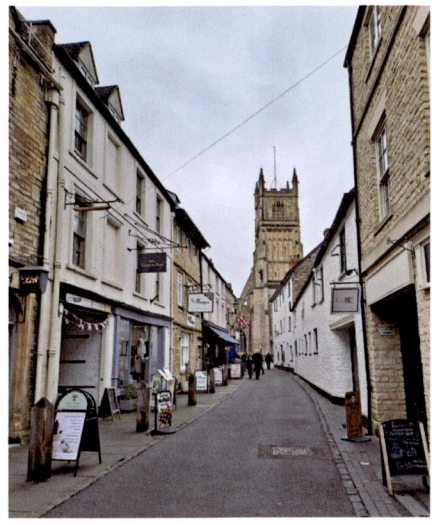

View up Black Jack Street, Cirencester, to the Church of St John the Baptist.

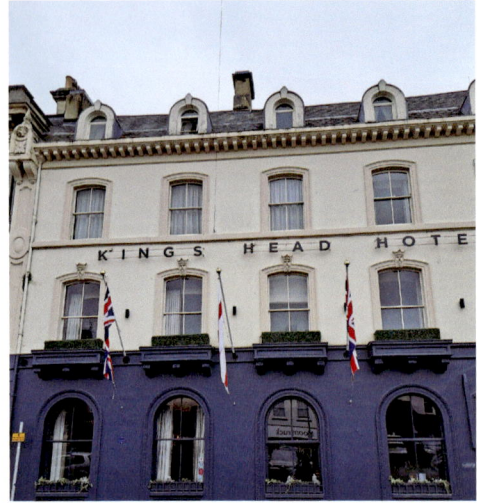

Kings Head Hotel, Cirencester.

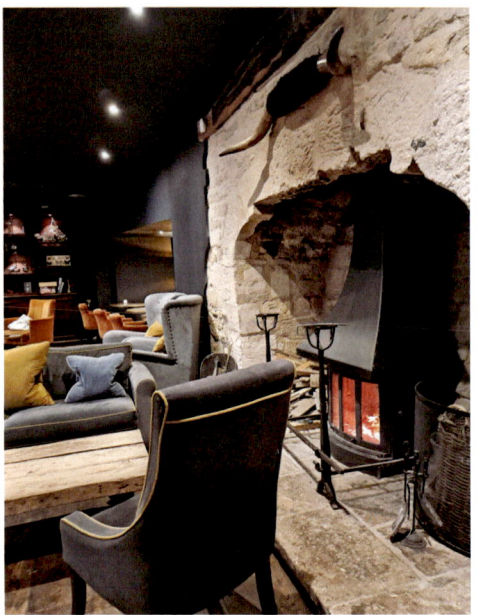

Kings Head Hotel lounge area, Cirencester.

The Fleece Inn

This traditional coaching inn with original oak beams and log fires has a history going back to 1651. Following defeat at the Battle of Worcester that year the young prince Charles (later King Charles II) fled from Cromwell's army and is believed to have used the building as a hiding place. Staff have seen the apparitions of an old woman and a Cavalier in the corridors of the hotel. Reports have emerged of several strange events in the building, including the sound of phantom footsteps, the sight of boxes flying off desks, and chairs falling over with no obvious explanation.

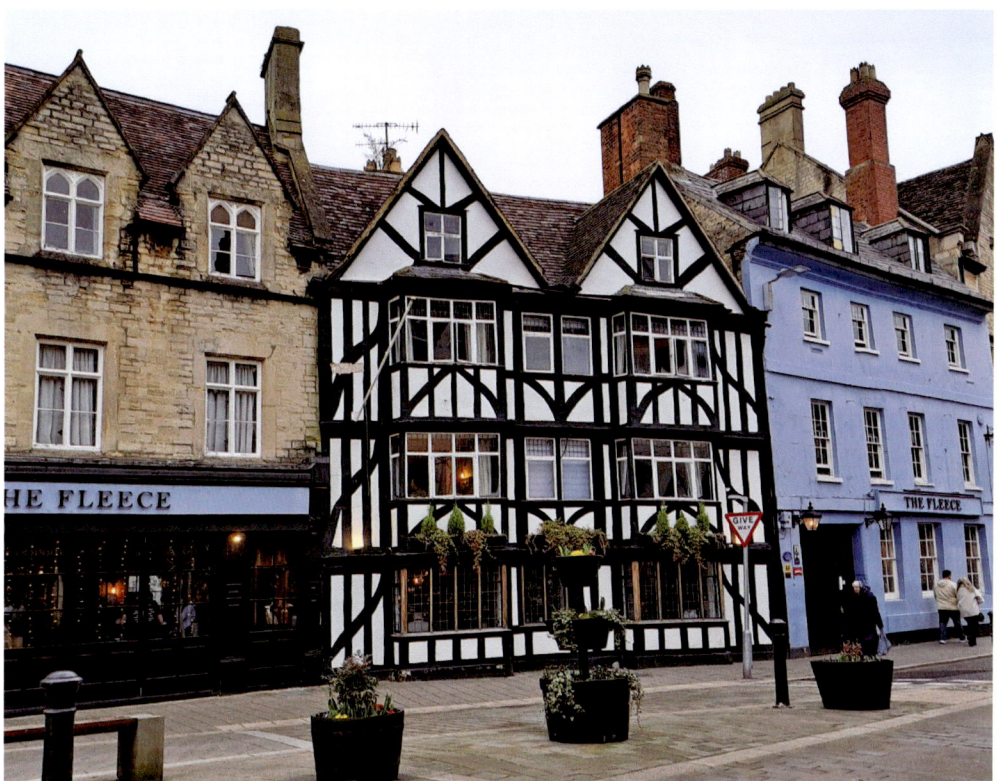

The Fleece, Cirencester.

Powell's Church of England Primary School

The unearthly appearance of 'a young girl,' described as having 'long brown hair and a full-length white petticoat' has been noted a number of times at around one o'clock in the morning, running between the two old buildings of this eighteenth-century school. This was reported in the *Wilts and Gloucestershire Standard* on 29 October 2014.

Some believe the girl to be Rebecca Powell, the founder of the school, who lived during the eighteenth century and who left the bequest which supported the school. Former pupils of Powell's School assert that 'the old schoolhouse was always rumoured to be haunted'.

The Powell family were great benefactors of Cirencester in the 1700s. Rebecca's husband Thomas in his will of 1718 and Rebecca in her will of 1722 left a large amount of money for charity in the town and local area. Thomas's bequest supported the Blue School for Boys and Rebecca's was used for the Yellow School for Girls. The two schools were amalgamated in 1876 under the name Powell's School. A link between the school and the parish church has been in place since 1714. Rebecca not only set up the original school here, but she also aided the foundations for several schools in the area to ensure the poorest could get an education.

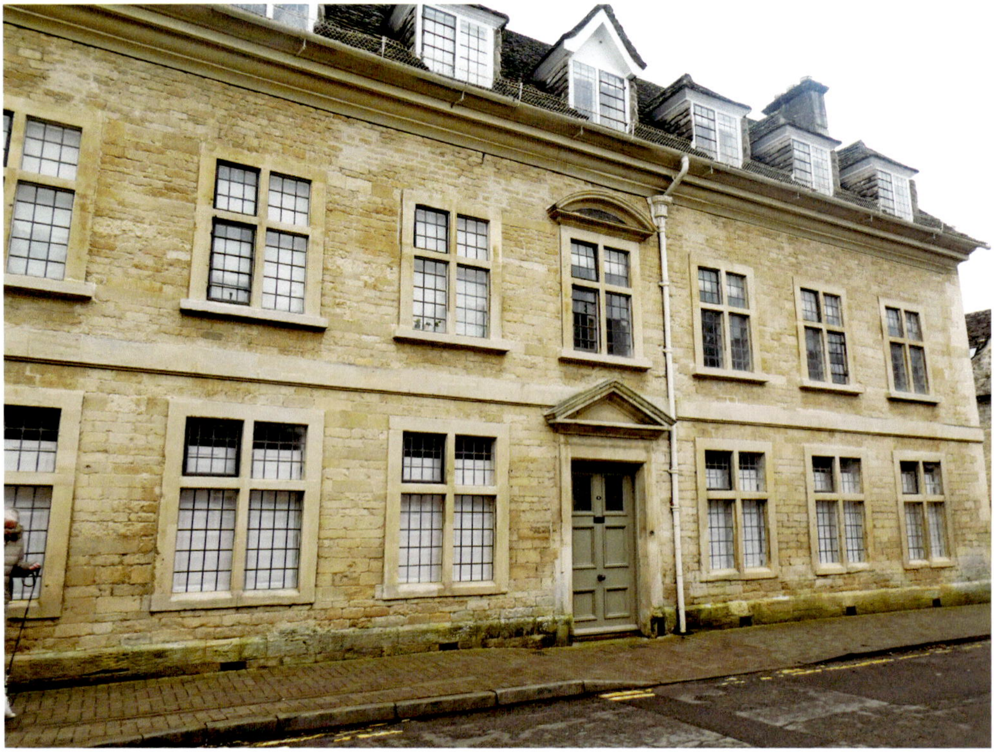

Powell's School, Cirencester. (Courtesy of Jamie Robinson)

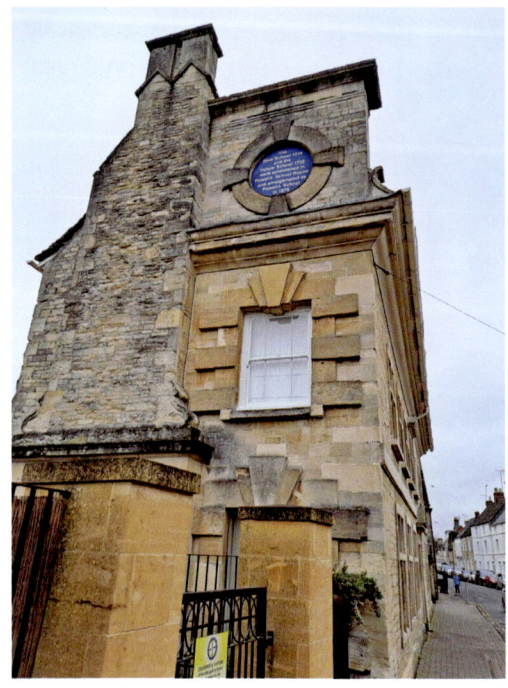

Powell's School side view, Cirencester.

8

Nympsfield and Surrounds

Woodchester Mansion

pale ghosts
Faintly besiege us

Henry VI Part I, Act 1, Scene 2

Woodchester Mansion stands deep in its south Gloucestershire valley today as 'an unfinished Gothic masterpiece'. Visitors liken their entry into the building to stepping into a time machine, and scores of people who have been inside for extended periods of time claim to have experienced at least one unexplainable event. Many of these stem from the time when the Ducie family owned and lived in the Georgian mansion that previously existed on this site. Uncanny sights and sounds attributable to the time of the Ducies' ownership have been reported in the kitchen, where a disembodied female voice singing traditional Irish tunes has been heard on several occasions, while several describe a shadowy man crouching in the corner apparently hiding from someone.

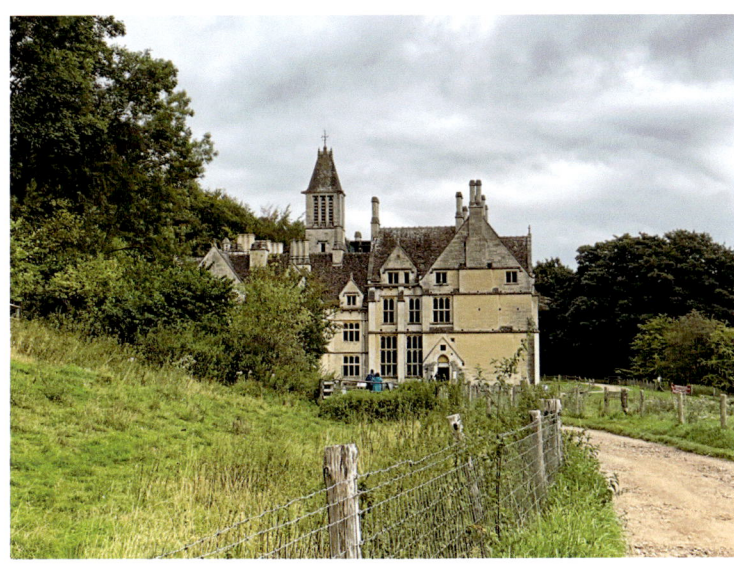

Approaching Woodchester Mansion. (Courtesy of Jamie Robinson)

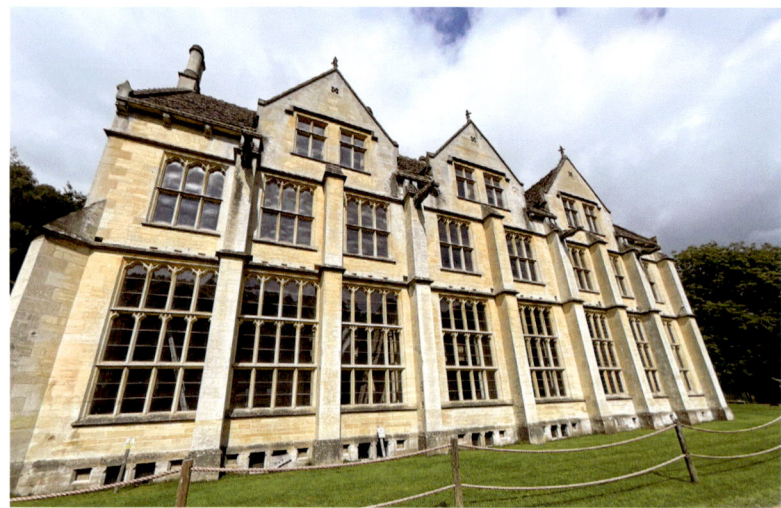

Woodchester Mansion south wall. (Courtesy of Jamie Robinson)

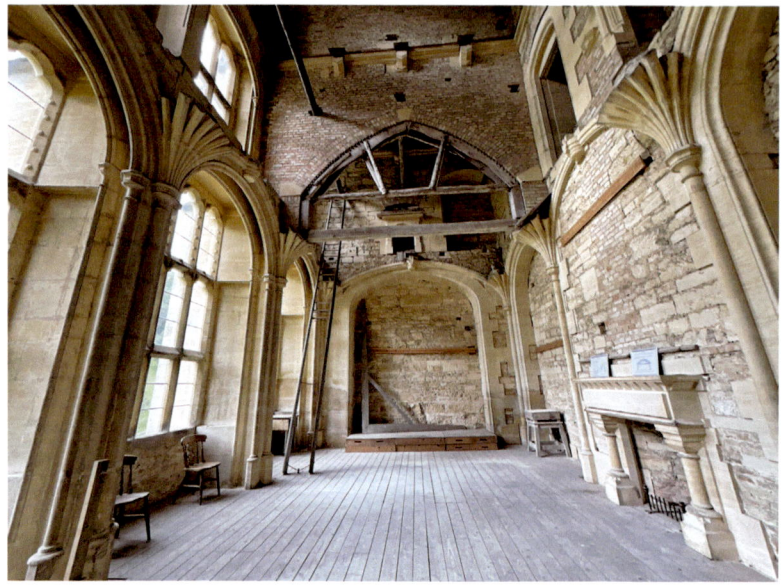

Unfinished dining room, Woodchester Mansion. (Courtesy of Jamie Robinson)

Such is the interest in weird happenings in the building, that groups with an interest in the paranormal rent it for observations. Chris Howley, who lives in Gloucester, supervises late-night vigils in the mansion. Sightings include a phantom horseman, an aggressive female and a floating head, so the mansion's night-time tours may not be 'for the faint-hearted.' Many of the visitors' experiences including those of Chris himself are detailed in his booklet *Ghosts of Woodchester Mansion*. These experiences include feelings of being watched in the cellar and apparitions of numerous people in various rooms and corridors of the mansion along with poltergeist phenomena, sounds of running footsteps, and drops in temperature.

The story behind the origins of the mansion centres upon the perfectionism and religious fervour of one man, the Roman Catholic convert William Leigh. William

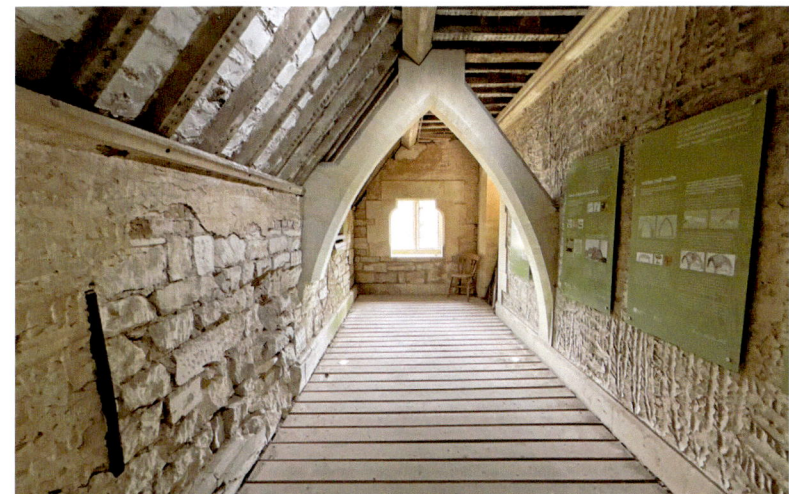

Top floor of Woodchester Mansion. (Courtesy of Jamie Robinson)

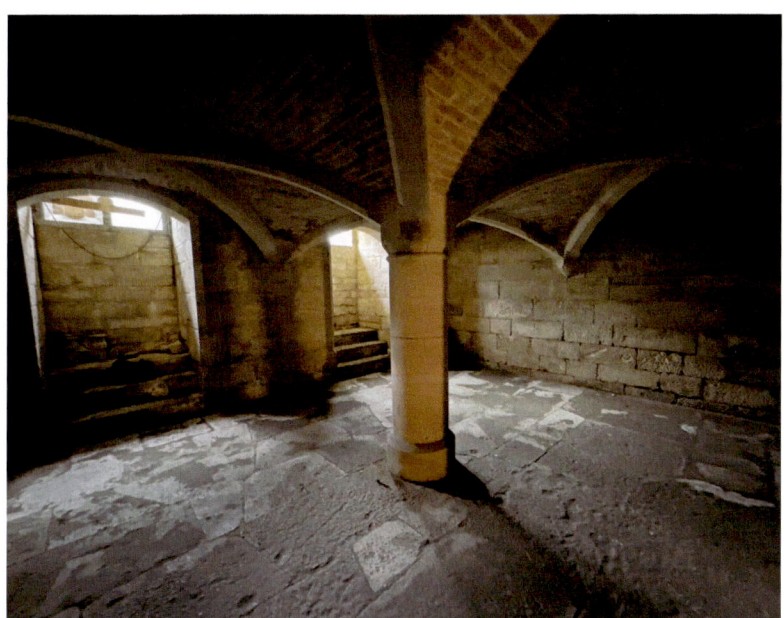

Cellar, Woodchester Mansion. (Courtesy of Jamie Robinson)

had moved from Staffordshire to Gloucestershire with plans to establish a Catholic centre in the villages of Nympsfield and Woodchester, in which aim he succeeded. The mansion was, for him, a grand project he embarked upon with ideals of architectural and artistic perfection, but which he had not completed at the time of his death in 1873. His son, Willie, now found himself responsible for the mansion but could not afford to complete and maintain it. It is possible that William preferred an incomplete but flawless building to a complete but imperfect structure. Haunting stories started because workmen departed so abruptly and left their tools behind, but as previously mentioned many of those stories derive from the Ducie family's period of occupation, for William and his family never lived there.

The Ducie family's earlier Georgian mansion had been completed in 1750, and it was called Spring Park. In *The Ghosts of Woodchester Mansion*, Chris Howley relates the rumoured tale of the second Earl of Ducie who, in 1840, held a decadent party here to celebrate his being made a duke. However, the festivities came to an abrupt halt when the duke went to take his place at the head of the dining table only to find his seat occupied by the ghost of his father. Shocked, he ran from the mansion and refused to return. He put the house and estate on the market, but it was not until five years later that he sold it to William Leigh of Staffordshire, in 1845.

Having purchased Spring Park and arrived in south Gloucestershire, William lived with his family in an enlarged gardeners' cottage on the estate. It was thirteen years before he began his building project, inspired by architect Pugin and his passion for the Gothic style. Grand houses had private chapels in Victorian times, and so he included a magnificent chapel. However, William would never have wished for or approved the interest current day visitors have in the chapel: it's said to be particularly spiritually active. The ghostly image of a stubby little man is frequently spotted standing the doorway, whom many consider to be probably a disappointed stonemason. Several visitors to the chapel have complained about being struck by flying pebbles which the little man may or may not be responsible for.

The mansion hosts a diverse array of unearthly residents: some of those reported include frightened children near the original stone-crafted bathroom on the first floor; a young woman named Elizabeth who was murdered; and a young girl who fell off a platform into the reception area whilst exploring the house with her friend.

In 1938, the last of William's grandchildren finally settled the fate of the unfinished house by selling it to Barnwood House Trust, and it was sold on again after the Second World War, then leased for a number of years. Following that it slid into oblivion for nearly three decades, used as a spooky adventure playground by local schoolchildren. In 1987 Stroud District Council bought the property and thirty acres of land, and later leased it to the charitable Woodchester Mansion Trust, founded in 1989. The mansion now hosts many different groups: schools in stone craftsmanship, students and admirers of nineteenth-century Gothic architecture, paranormal investigators,

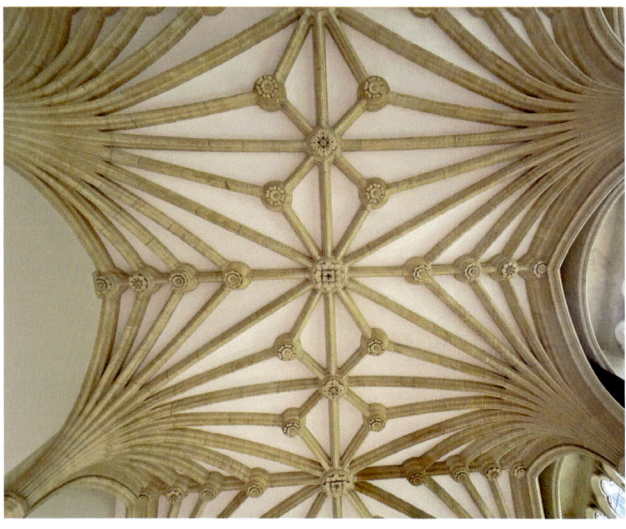

Ceiling of the drawing room, Woodchester Mansion, completed for a visit from Cardinal Vaughan in 1894. (Courtesy of Jamie Robinson)

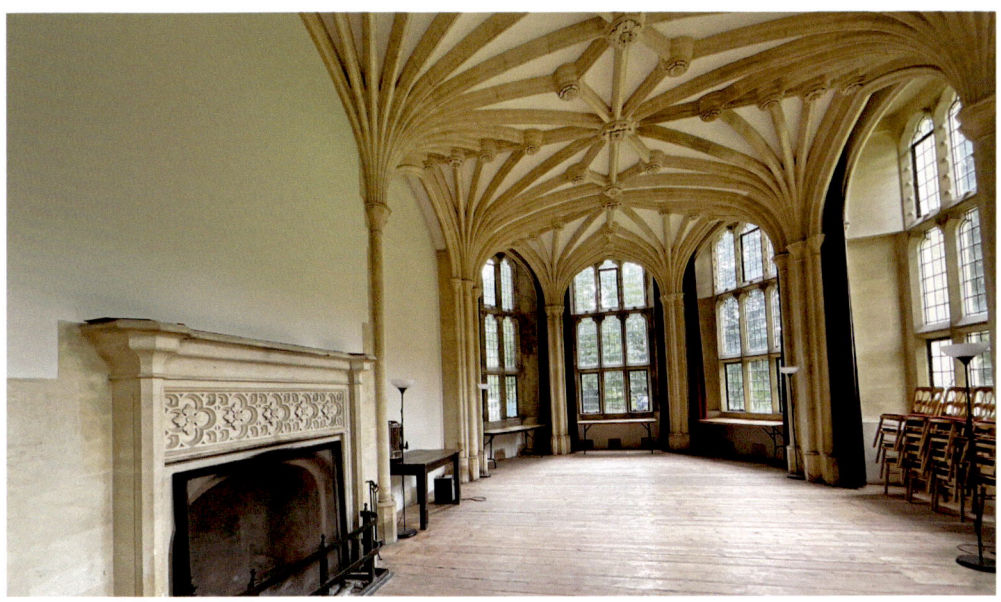

Drawing room, Woodchester Mansion. (Courtesy of Jamie Robinson)

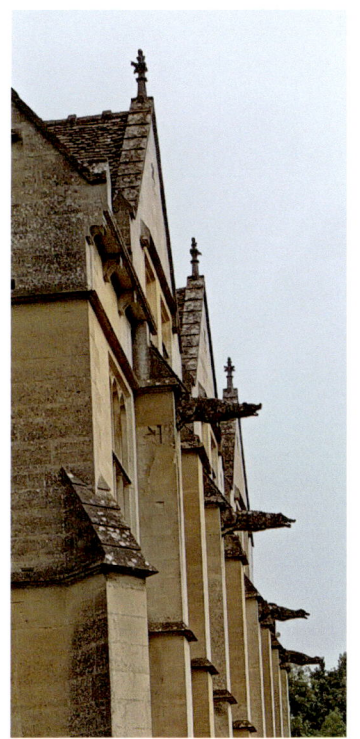

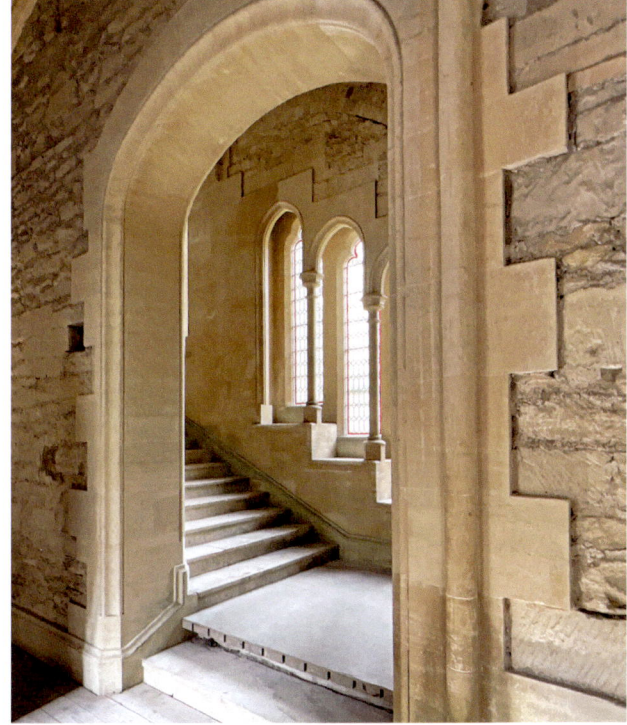

Above left: Gargoyles on south wall, Woodchester Mansion.

Above right: Staircase, Woodchester Mansion. (Courtesy of Jamie Robinson)

and tourists and film makers, while the only finished room, the Drawing Room, is used for concerts and conferences.

A large colony of bats roost in the attics, protected and nurtured as an endangered species, and visible on screens in the first-floor Bat Observatory. The mansion hosts 550 adult lesser horseshoe bats and 180 adult greater horseshoe bats. In addition, there is a Pipistrelle colony of ninety adults, and small numbers of brown long-eared bats and serotines. In July when the young are present, the bat colony exceeds 1,000 individuals. The mansion, therefore, is well used and enjoyed by many, including the bats, who are very grateful for their warm, comfortable home in the attics.

Two Ancient Burial Chambers

Give them burial as beseems their worth

Henry VI Part 1, Act 4, Scene 7

Uley Long Barrow (Hetty Pegler's Tump)

Uley Long Barrow was built over 5,500 years ago and discovered and excavated in 1821. A Roman man was buried in the earth of the mound, but no researchers have yet discovered why. Local legend tells of the occasional reappearance of a Roman soldier who is seen standing around the tump in the mist, his plumed helmet and shield clearly visible.

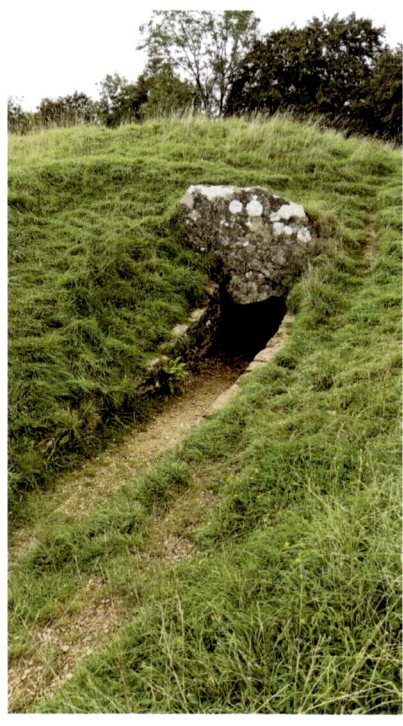

Uley Long Barrow.

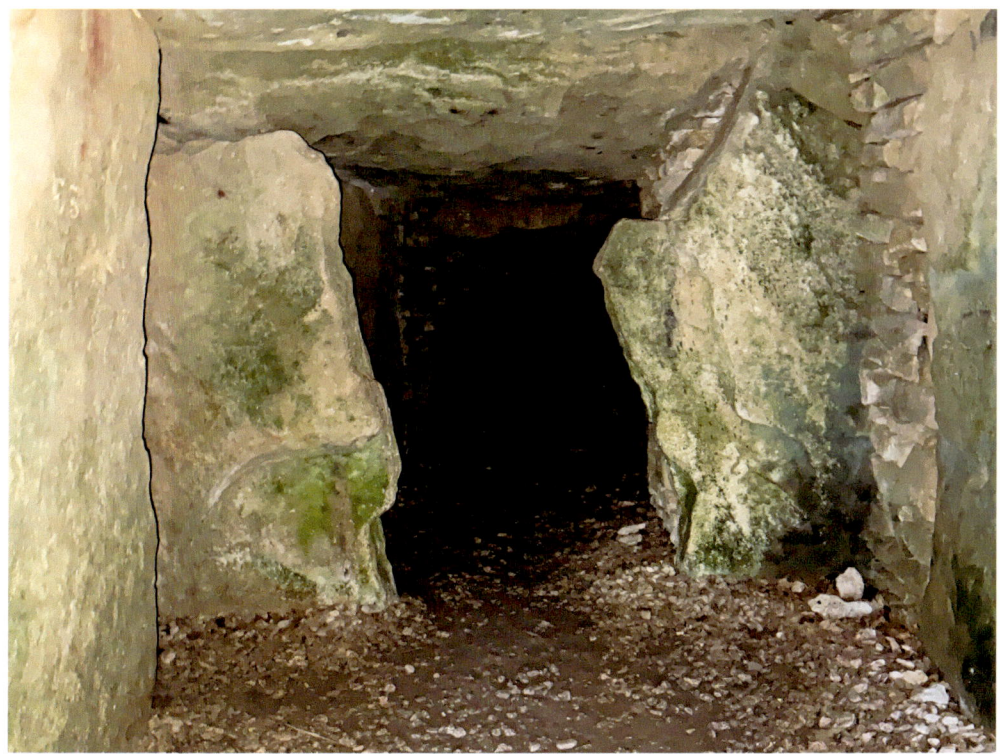

Close-up of the entrance of Uley Long Barrow. (Courtesy of Jamie Robinson)

The two seventeenth-century owners of the field, Hester and Henry Pegler, inspired the barrow's unusual alternative name of Hetty Pegler's Tump. It is a neolithic burial mound used by the people of that era to lay their family and loved ones to rest in a ceremonial fashion. Visitors today find a multi-chambered burial round rather than a long barrow. The barrow was further investigated in 1854 and 2011. The remains of twenty-two individuals from the neolithic era have been discovered during excavations along with pieces of pottery and a perforated boar's tusk pendant which was discovered during the excavations of 1854.

Nympsfield Long Barrow (North of Uley)

Another neolithic burial mound may be found along the ridge of the Coaley Peak viewpoint near Dursley. This barrow has long been surrounded by legends and odd stories. The stones of the structure were believed to be able to move around on their own and on certain nights would roll down the hill to the valley then back up again. At least one tale exists of a local man who took a slab from the barrow to use as building material and regretted it, towing it back up the hill and reinstating it, after hearing terrifying screams every night the stones stood in his wall.

This long barrow is uncovered and open to the elements. Excavations were first carried out in 1862, then in 1937 and lastly in 1974. During these excavations the remains of at least thirteen human skeletons have been recovered.

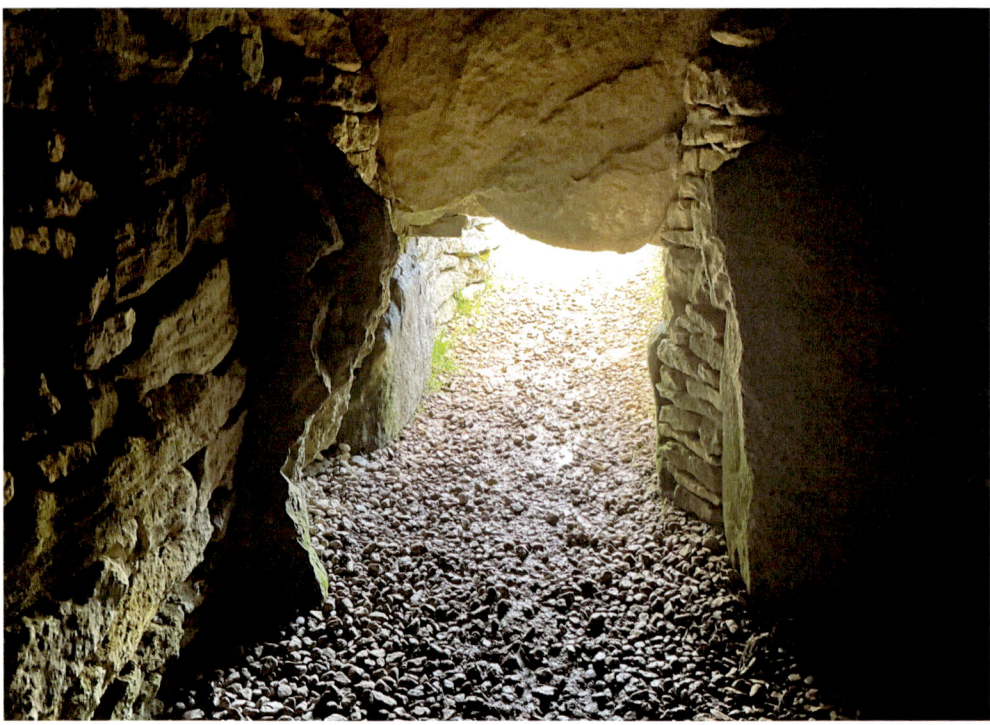

View from inside the burial chamber of Uley Long Barrow. (Courtesy of Jamie Robinson)

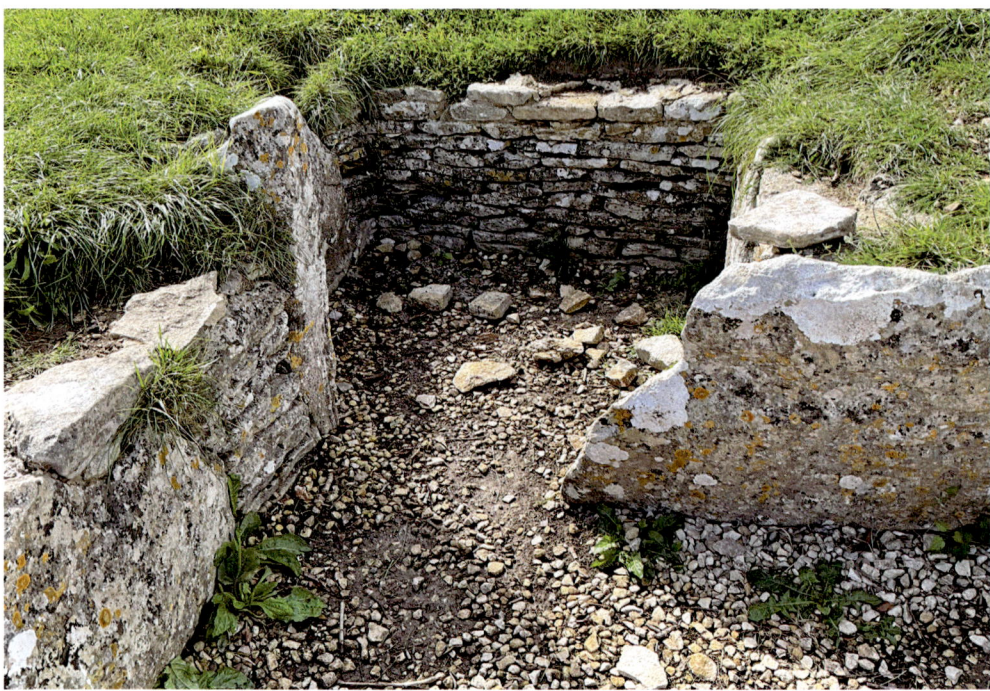

Entrance to Nympsfield Long Barrow. (Courtesy of Jamie Robinson)

9

Lydney and Surrounds

St Briavels Castle

Our king...
Comes hunting this way to disport himself.

Henry VI Part III, Act 4, Scene 5

This Norman castle was built in the twelfth century for the Crown, serving as a border stronghold and a royal hunting lodge for King John (1199–1216). As an important royal castle on the frontier with Wales, it became the residence of the Warden of the Forest of Dean.

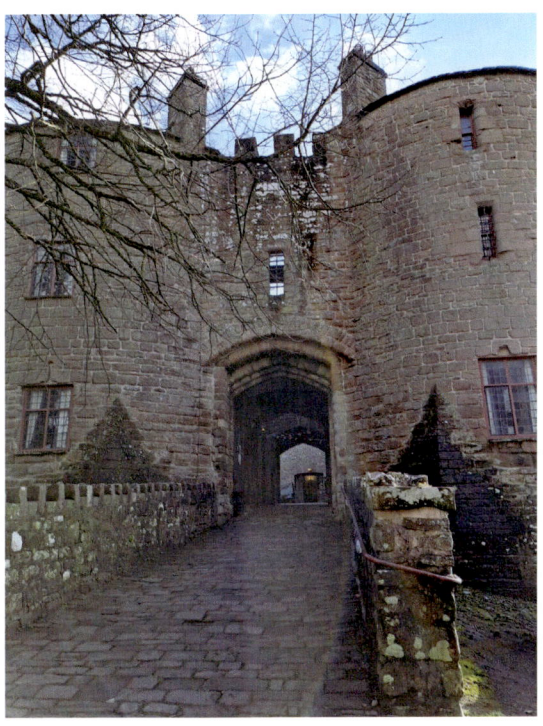

St Briavels Castle drawbridge.

As for the Celtic saint who gave both town and castle its name, nothing is known for sure; Briavel was only first recorded in 1130. But it's likely his character had little in common with the activities within the castle that took his name. The castle witnessed many a murder during its heyday in the twelfth century, and this fact has given rise to numerous unsettling events. Attendees of overnight vigils at the castle are said to have heard the pitiful cries of an unseen baby, felt invisible hands tugging at clothes and the sensation of someone gripping at a visitor's throat.

During the reign of Edward I (1272–1307) thousands of crossbow bolts were produced and the castle became an arsenal for locally produced weaponry. Edward I, too, built the massive twin-towered gatehouse in 1292. With the conquest of Wales completed by the end of the fifteenth century, the castle lost its military function and its importance declined rapidly. Unused buildings were demolished in 1680. Thereafter and up until 1842, the castle was used as a harsh and overcrowded Debtors' Prison. The inscriptions of many hapless prisoners may be found on the walls of their cells. Fully restored in the mid-twentieth century, the castle is owned by English Heritage and now operates as a youth hostel, with the moat, garden and inner-bailey area open to the public.

Many ghost sightings have been reported over the years, some happening on a regular basis such as the sound of phantom horses' hooves through the gatehouse corridor. Often visitors to the castle, upon being let through the main gates, turn round to see the person who let them in, only to find nobody there.

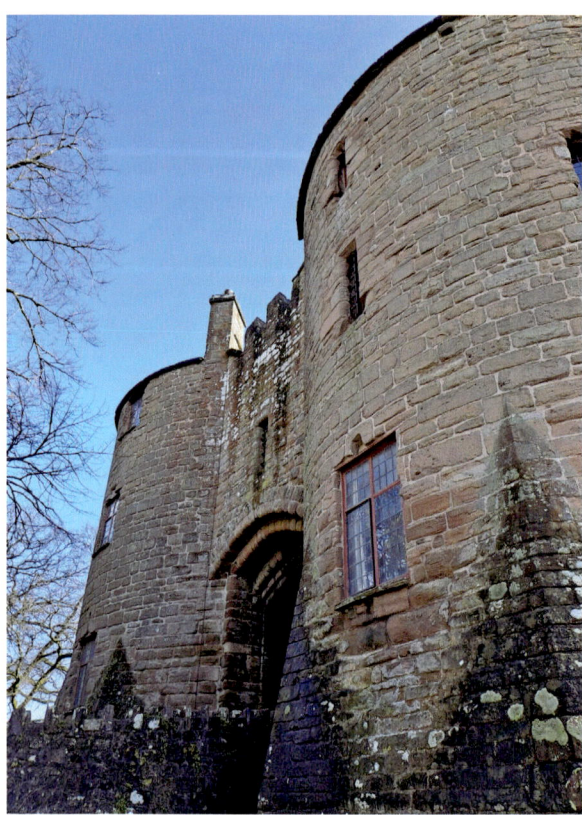

Main entrance, St Briavels Castle.

10

Berkeley Castle

Bolingbroke: How far is it, my lord, to Berkeley now?
North: I am a stranger here in Gloucestershire:
These high wild hills and rough uneven ways
Draw out our miles…
Percy: There stands the castle, by yon tuft of trees.

Richard II, Act 2, Scene 3

Berkeley Castle stands in a perfect strategic location overlooking the Welsh hills across the River Severn, on one of the main routes between Bristol and Gloucester. In the twelfth century the earlier wooden structure stood here, then Robert Fitzharding was given permission to replace the wooden castle with the stone keep, which has maintained its formidable presence for nearly 900 years. A long and dramatic history has unfolded within the castle including an event which soon took centre stage in the imaginations of many: the death of King Edward II. The association of the castle with the miserable end of this unpopular monarch has given rise to the grimmest in a litany of many odd tales surrounding Berkeley. Edward was probably murdered there in 1327, but contemporary historians offer three different accounts of the circumstances.

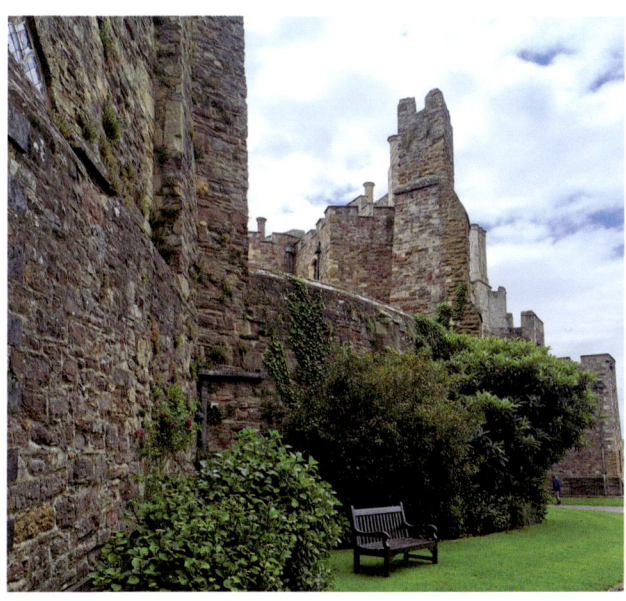

View of Berkeley Castle.

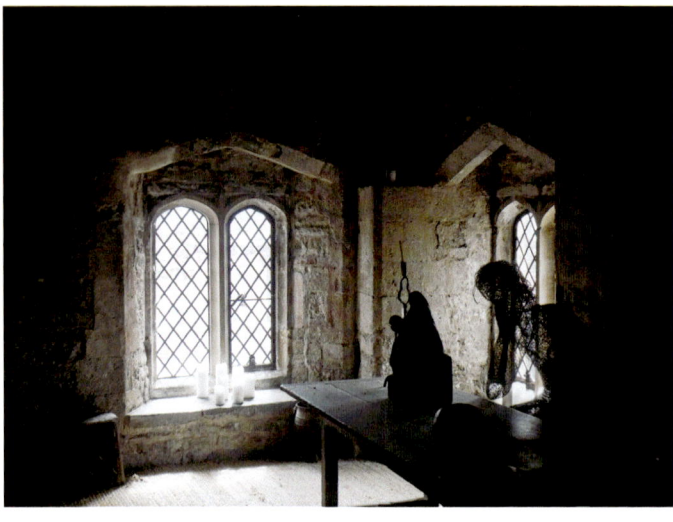

Edward II's cell, Berkeley Castle. (Courtesy of Jamie Robinson, with thanks to Mr Michael Berkeley of Berkeley Castle)

Edward, betrayed by his wife Isabella and her lover Roger Mortimer, was imprisoned in the cellar guard room next to the dungeon which at that time had an interconnecting door. During Edward's period of imprisonment, they would throw the carcasses of dead animals into the dungeon, which would decompose and emit noxious fumes. The foul air would filter through into the guardroom, which they hoped would infect him with disease, so he'd become sick and die of what they could call 'natural causes'. But that didn't work, so on 21 September 1327 Roger Mortimer sent instructions to have him murdered.

Edward's captors wanted to kill him in such a way that there would be no signs of violence on his body. It is most likely he was suffocated – unless, as some historians believe, he was rescued, and the man buried in the elaborate tomb in Gloucester Cathedral is actually one of the guards who got killed in the course of Edward's escape. In that alternative scenario, it is suggested that Edward went to Ireland until after all the fuss died down, then later travelled to Europe where he lived out his life as a hermit in a Northern Italian hermitage. According to present knowledge and research, it seems most likely he was murdered but not in the gruesome way often claimed. Nevertheless, we await further evidence to come to light as a result of the historians' research.

Perhaps the screams that are said to be heard throughout the castle on the anniversary of Edward's death may have another origin within the history of Berkeley; or maybe they are connected with Edward after all; currently, nobody can be sure.

Other unsettling tales also emerge from the castle's history, and one of these is focussed upon the great hall, built in the mid-fourteenth century. The minstrels' gallery is 500 years old and two of the castle's ghost stories relate to this gallery. In 1728, Dicky Pearce, the last court jester in England, was performing for the guests here during the visit of his master, the Earl of Suffolk. But during the evening, as Dicky entertained with acrobatics and jokes, he went too far with one of his jokes against an important guest. He was chased up the stairs to the gallery, overbalanced, and fell. Did he fall or was he pushed? Whatever the answer to that question, he died a few days

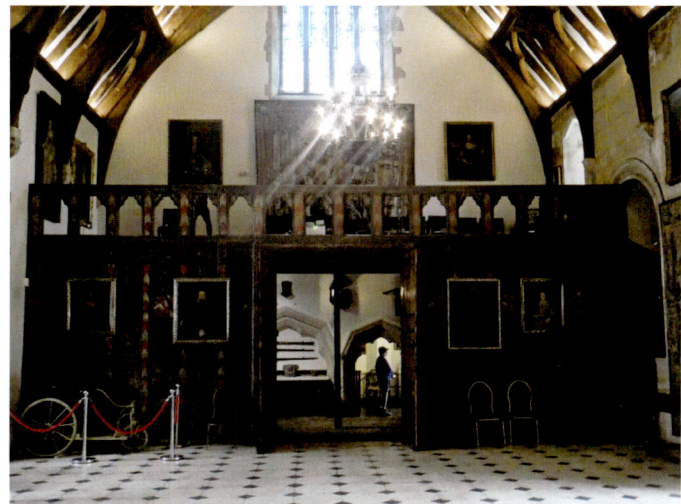

Minstrels' gallery in the great hall, Berkeley Castle. (Courtesy of Jamie Robinson, with thanks to Mr Michael Berkeley of Berkeley Castle)

later of his injuries. His tomb is in the Church of St Mary in Berkeley village. There are those who claim to have seen his spectral form falling from the gallery.

Charles Berkeley, current owner of the castle, tells me, too, of 'the lady in white seen going up the minstrels' gallery stairs, and a monk/priest in the Morning Room'.

The room he refers to is on the upper floor of the castle, and it was formerly used as a chapel. The castle history guide told us that when a chapel in a grand country home was deconsecrated and converted to a family room, it was customary to replace a removed altar with a piece of furniture carved with a pagan subject – as demonstrated here in the shape of the pagan cabinet. Lord Berkeley also put a fireplace in, and he would sit in this room writing his letters. Two fine books are displayed in this room: a very early King James Bible from the 1640s and in another cabinet an Antiphonal, a book of antiphons, or medieval church chants; this book dates back to 1400. That distant branch of the family always remained Catholic all the way through the Reformation.

Our guide stood in front of the pagan cabinet and informed us the Morning Room is 'the most haunted in the castle. Many visitors have told me, "We're very conscious of the spirits when we're here". This is the room they come to. I was showing the castle to a group a few weeks ago. One of the group said, "I have to tell you there is something behind you right now".'

Charles Berkeley also told me of his mother's two stories about 'the ladies in the Inner Bailey in Victorian costume who disappeared in front of her, and the haunted Bow Room (bedroom) where she felt someone breathing down her neck whilst making a bed'.

Back once more outside the great hall, we may find a flight of steps leading down to the beer cellar. The smaller barrels here hold 450 gallons. In one year, 19,000 gallons of beer was consumed at Berkeley Castle. The cellar does have a strong atmosphere, and is considered to be particularly eerie, with visitors feeling a heavy presence and experiencing intense feelings of unease.

Tragic deaths do seem to cluster around the castle: besides the supposed manner of Edward II's demise, other tragedies here include the deaths of several children who fell

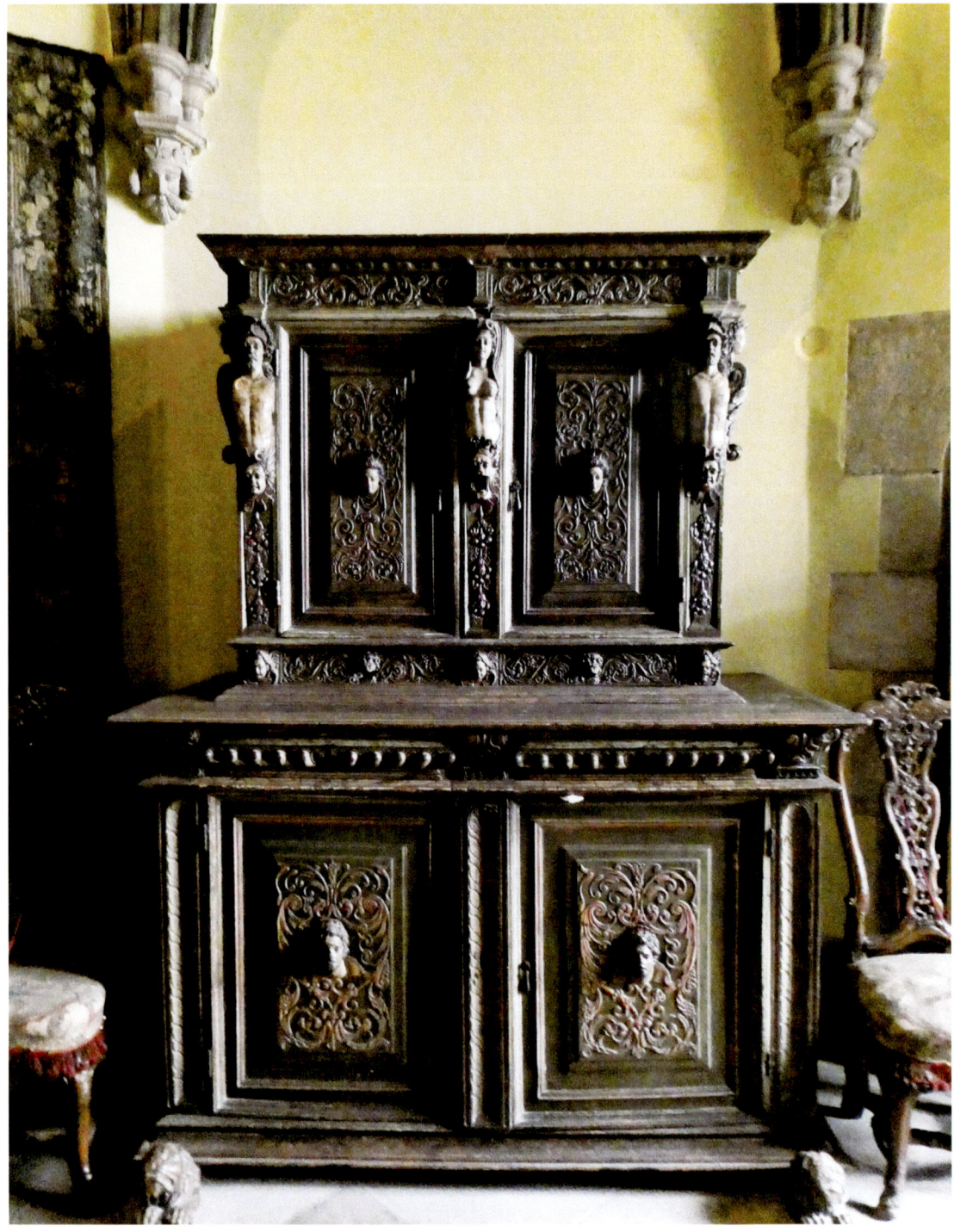

Pagan cabinet in the Morning Room, Berkeley Castle. (Courtesy of Jamie Robinson, with thanks to Mr Michael Berkeley of Berkeley Castle)

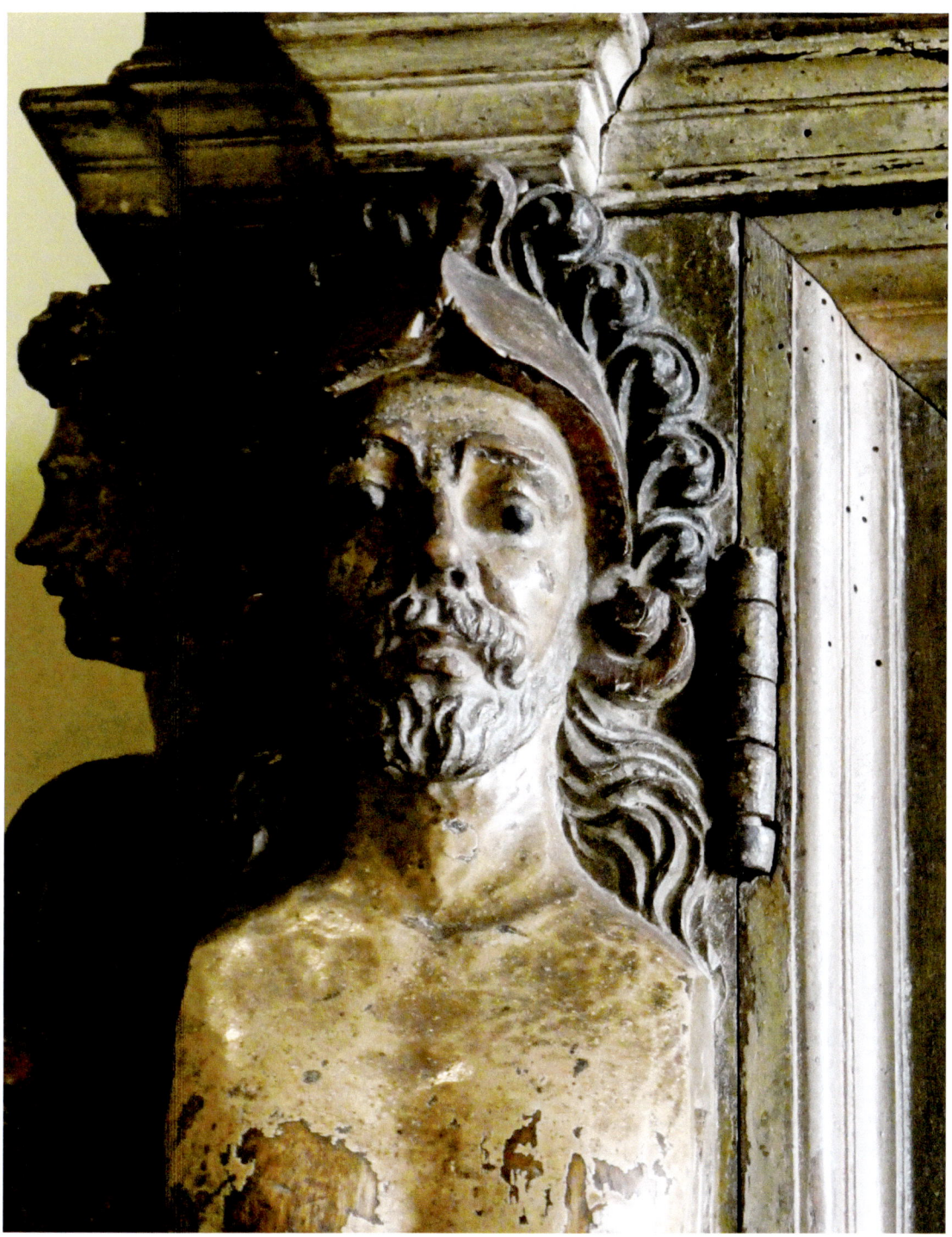

Detail of carving on the cabinet, Berkeley Castle. (Courtesy of Jamie Robinson, with thanks to Mr Michael Berkeley of Berkeley Castle)

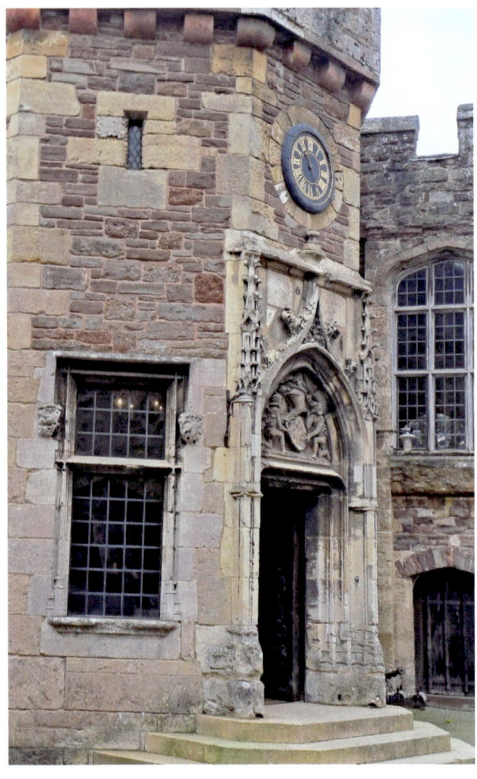

Doorway into the vestibule of the great hall, Berkeley Castle.

from the castle's towers, as well as the suicides of a number of residents. These events fuel the castle's haunted reputation, with numerous reports of paranormal activity throughout its history.

One of the most well-known spirits is the White Lady, referred to above by Charles Berkeley. Visitors have reported seeing this spectre often accompanied by a feeling of unease or a sudden drop in temperature. Other unearthly presences include the monk he mentioned as having been seen in the Morning Room, who is believed to be a former resident of the castle, and many have claimed to hear disembodied voices, footsteps, and whispers echoing throughout the castle. Some have even reported seeing shadowy figures roaming the halls. Another legend tells of a secret tunnel that runs beneath the castle connecting it to a nearby church. According to the story, this tunnel was used by a priest to escape persecution during the Reformation. These first-person accounts have only added to the castle's reputation as one of Britain's most haunted locations.

Berkeley Castle has a close association with many turning points of English history, and fortune has smiled upon the Berkeleys, despite their nefarious behaviour; they have held this castle for 900 years. For one family to hold a castle for that long is unique in English history. That comes from good luck as well as common sense, for when hovering on the edge of ruin and disgrace in the face of a tyrant monarch, as many an aristocratic family may have done in past centuries, most would have lost their castle right there; but the history of the Berkeleys always confirms that they got it back again.

11

Dursley and Surrounds

Owlpen Manor, Uley

Dark-working sorcerers that change the mind,
Soul-killing witches.

Comedy of Errors, Act 1, Scene 2

The mysterious-looking Owlpen Manor was originally owned by a family called Olepenne who lived here from 1100 until 1462 and adopted the owl as their symbol. This celebrated Cotswold property hides deep in a valley, together with its steeply terraced gardens full of topiary. To us it looks idyllic, but its varied history has included an owner who studied and practised sorcery in the attic, and a garden which a great landscape architect likened to 'a witch's coven'. Past writers about Owlpen have noted how you stumble across the house sideways in a remote valley behind a dripping barrier of yews, presenting a romantic view with an ancient garden. Sir Nicholas Mander, the present owner, told us: 'The garden cascades down the hillside in terraces in a rather Italianate style. Geoffrey Jellicoe told me... "you mustn't alter it". It has a medieval feeling, he said, "like a witch's coven".'

Sir Nicholas and his wife, Karen, purchased the house and estate from Francis Pagan in 1974. Sir Nicholas, highly knowledgeable about the history of the manor has published several books on the subject. He showed us around the property and the garden, sharing its stories and pointing out the Arts and Craft features and treasures within. Inevitably, a house of this age has its share of unearthly residents.

As Sir Nicholas said:

Old houses usually suggest ghost stories – and this is a dark secret house hidden in the valley. Stories abound of ... medieval monks escaping from the Dissolution of the Monasteries. There was an Abbey nearby. There is also ... a mischievous and lively little girl who plays around with things and runs up and down the back stairs. As for Queen Margaret of Anjou, she's said to revisit Owlpen on the eve of the Battle of Tewkesbury and she comes here because she spent her last happy night here; the next day her son was butchered at the battle and her husband was murdered a few days later. She retired in penury to France, so the story goes she wants to come back.

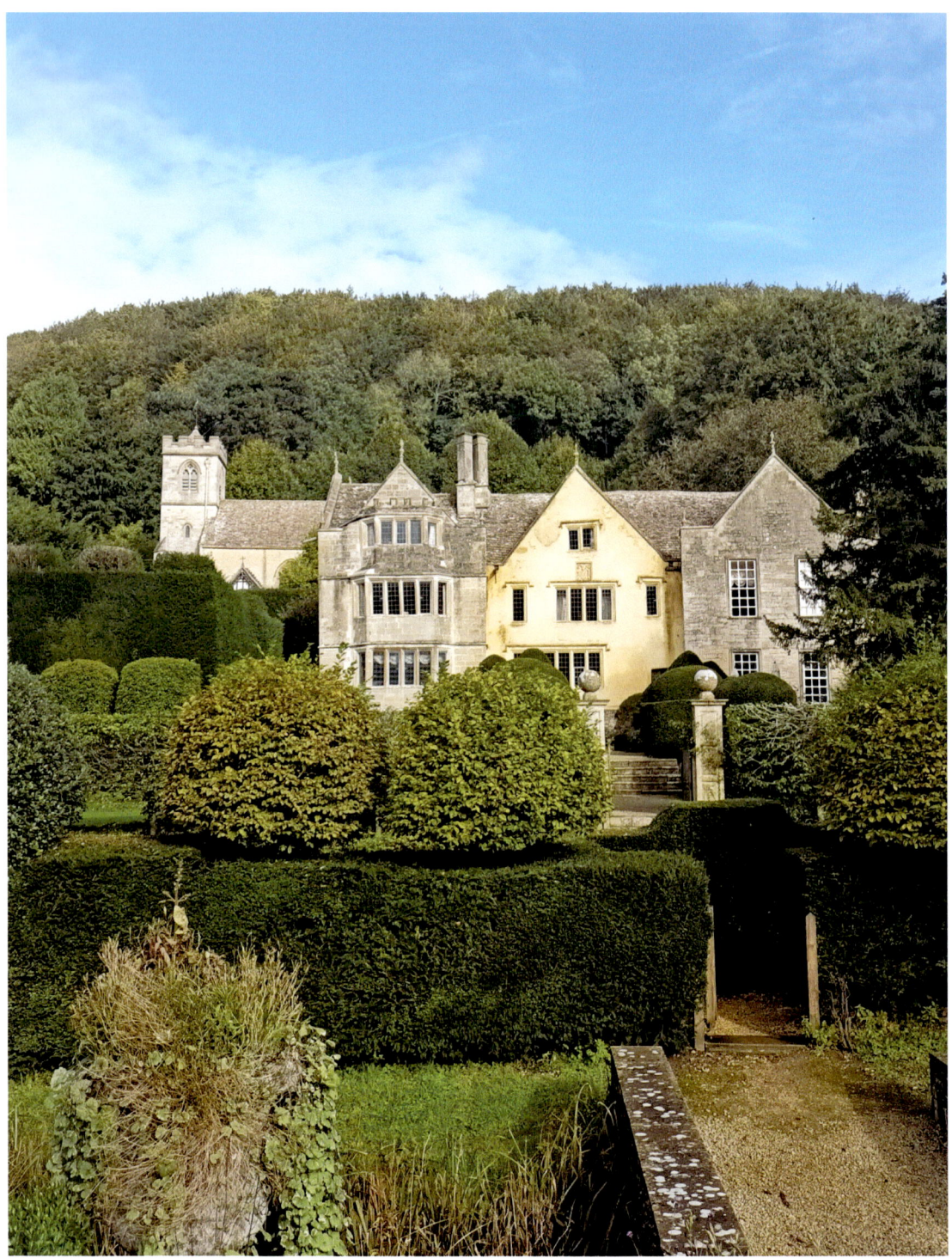

Owlpen Manor from the garden lookout.

Later, when Sir Nicholas's son Hugo took over the tour, he added: 'Queen Margaret stayed here on the night of 3 May 1471 ... She is seen standing by the bed, so I'm told by various clairvoyants and dowsers who've visited ... Many have described all sorts of eerie stories.'

Several past residents and guests claim to have sighted the ill-fated Queen. Some of these were Second World War evacuee children billeted by Mrs Barbara Bray who owned the house from 1926 to 1963. Sir Nicholas explains:

> Mrs Barbara Bray of Owlpen was the billeting officer for the east end of Birmingham, bringing evacuee children into local country houses. Some of the children asked about the beautiful dress she had been wearing the previous evening and when she said she didn't know what dress they meant, and actually she had not even been there, they described the dress as that typical of a high status lady in medieval times.

Author Francis Comstock relates this story:

> One night, in making her customary round, Barbara looked in to (check whether) the four children were sleeping. She found them all awake and excited; they told her of their visitor, 'a lovely lady with long sleeves and dress all trimmed with fur, and with a funny peaked hat that had a long veil hanging down behind', a description of such a costume as Queen Margaret might have worn, and of which the children must have been completely ignorant.

Sir Nicholas showed us into the Oak Parlour, noting that by early 1616 people were getting the idea of 'withdrawing rooms', offering more privacy; and the oak panels would be decorated with the liberal use of green and paintings of leaves. The graffiti on the left of the fireplace shows the date 1648. He said:

> Leaves keep out evil spirits from doors and windows, so they don't get into the house. There were many so-called witch marks in houses ... James I wrote books on demonology and witchcraft ... educated people were also overwhelmed by these things. Upstairs you see a lot of them around fireplaces. Often shoes were concealed in early houses which have been found and nobody quite knows the origins. The custom goes back a very long way, and people buried cats too in walls. Here you will find all sorts of things typical of a house of this period that is not a stately home: things you wouldn't find in the grander houses that succeeded them.

Covering the walls of Queen Margaret's Room we may see a rare historical treasure: the last complete set of early eighteenth-century painted linen cloths hanging in Britain in a private house. Owlpen was abandoned in the late 1700s, so no one thought to take them down, and they have remained in the house ever since. The pictures painted on these cloths tell the story of Joseph from Genesis in the Old Testament. 'These painted cloths lend age and spookiness to haunted rooms ... shoes have been found (hidden in strange places centuries ago) – good luck charms.'

Besides Margaret of Anjou re-living her last happy night in this world it is reported that Owlpen Manor has other ghosts. St Nicholas's wife, Lady Karen, says: 'My father saw the ghost of Margaret. The way to cope with being on your own in this house is to talk to them.'

A black monk is seen 'malingering in the older, east wing'; 'a wizard/alchemist' makes his presence felt in the attic, and a mischievous child is heard running up and down stairs in the night, disturbing people's sleep. A team of paranormal investigators visited Owlpen Manor in March 2004 and filmed in the attic, accompanied by one of the owners' dogs. They reported an oppressive atmosphere, light anomalies at the door, and poltergeist phenomena such as a book flying out of the bookcase and hitting one of the crew in the back.

The association is with Thomas Daunt the Seventh, variously described as a magician, sorcerer and 'a wizard and alchemist … who dabbled in the black arts.' He was lord of the manor in Georgian times; the Daunt family had inherited the property in 1463, and lived at Owlpen for three hundred years, until the male line failed in 1803. By 1807, author T. D. Fosbrooke was describing the house as 'half dilapidated and overrun with ivy', neglected by Thomas Daunt's daughter whose primary focus was the family property of her husband in Ireland.

But it is also suggested that the presence in the attic could also be 'the family tutor who raised the devil, wrote books on sorcery and was found dead in his chair'.

These ideas have probably been derived from books discovered in the attic which belonged to Thomas and indicate he was involved in black magic. It was claimed:

> After his death, the sealed room in which his books and papers had been kept for many years was said to be haunted. Those books and papers were thought to be so dangerous that the local parson was sent for and did destroy some of them; as they were burning, birds flew out of them.

Owlpen is now in the hands of careful guardians, its rich history honoured along with the works of artists and craftworkers. One of the former owners was Norman Jewson, who undertook a considerable amount of sympathetic restoration to honour the Arts and Crafts links in their home. The Mander family continue to preserve their artistic inheritance today, so the future of this beautiful house is well secured.

12

Littledean

Ghosts, wandering here and there,
Troop home

A Midsummer Night's Dream, Act 3, Scene 2

Littledean Jail Museum

Upon opening in 1791, Littledean Jail admitted its first prisoner: one Joseph Marshall, aged nineteen, who was convicted of stealing a spade. He was the first of thousands to be brutally punished for such crimes and was followed by scores of men, women and children. Many unearthly experiences are reported on the site. Visitors frequently report the sound of children chattering and playing with one another in areas where no children are present; and occasionally, the phantom of a man in a green uniform loitering outside what was once the prison courtroom. He then returns to the courtroom, passing through the wall.

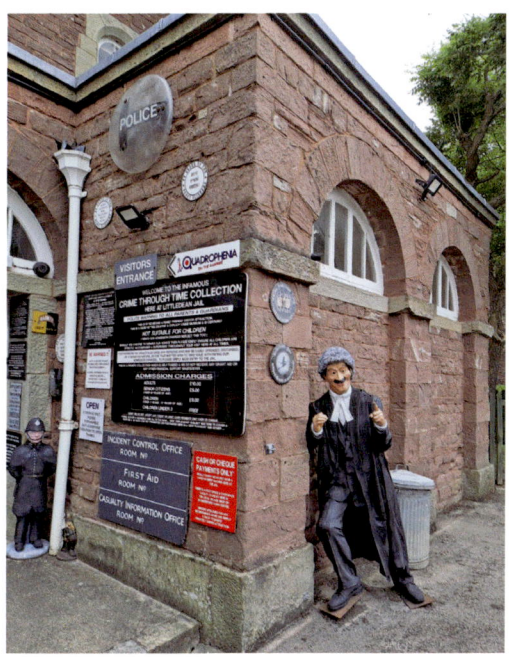

Littledean Jail Museum entrance.

From 1854, the building was used as a police station, remand prison and petty session court. A notable trial took place at the Jail in 1906: that of Ellen Hayward, Cinderford wise woman, the last person charged with witchcraft in Gloucestershire. Ellen was a respected herbalist, and she was tried for the crime of 'not being a witch.' She would often walk through the Forest of Dean to St Anthony's Well near Littledean, and she also practised her craft near May Hill (now in the ownership of the National Trust). May Hill is considered by many to be a magical place, a haunt of wood spirits, a magnet to pagans and an abode of 'guardians of dreams'.

Ellen's charge was 'pretending to be a witch to deceive James Davis.' The case was dismissed, and Ellen was able to continue practising her craft of herbal healing. She is buried in the churchyard in Cinderford; her grave is opposite that of the judge who tried her in court for witchcraft. The Jail continued operating as a magistrates' court until 1985.

One of the old jail doors, secured by two iron bolts, is known to open by itself. Visitors have also reported the sound of footsteps through the upstairs part of the prison when no-one else is in the building. Today Littledean Jail is open to the public and is occupied by the Crime Through Time Collection.

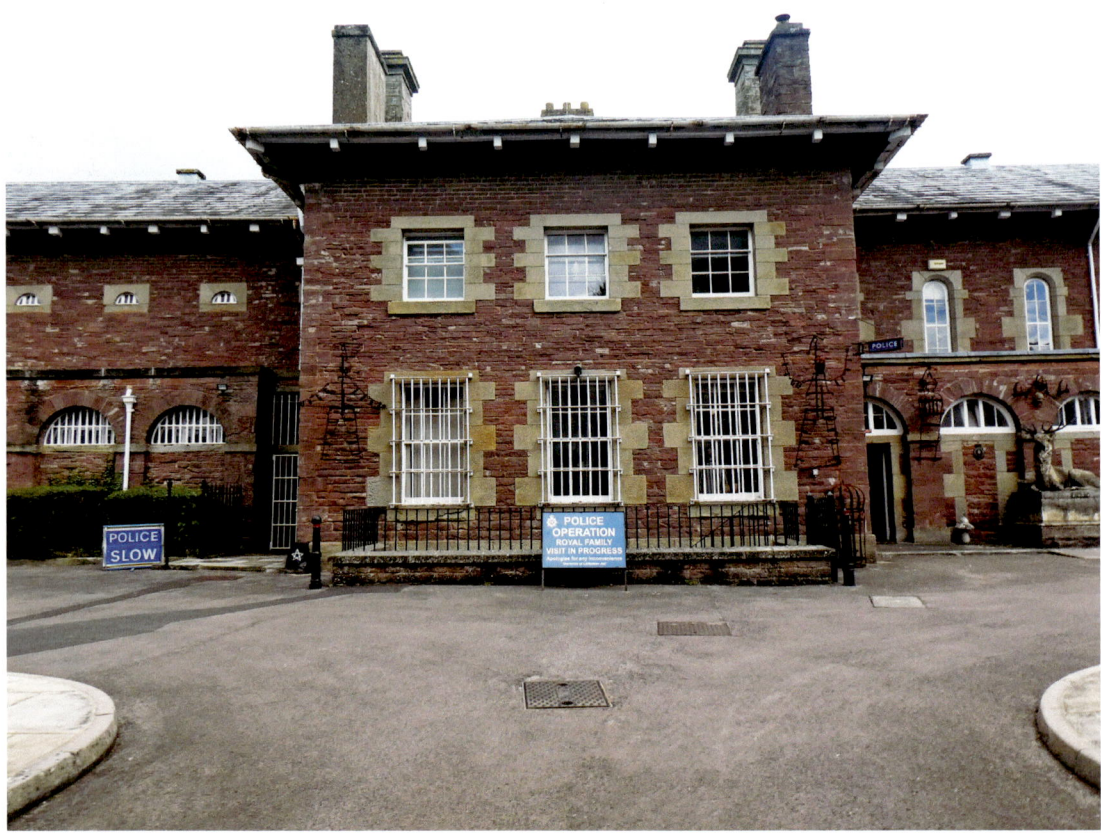

Littledean Jail Museum courtyard. (Courtesy of Jamie Robinson)

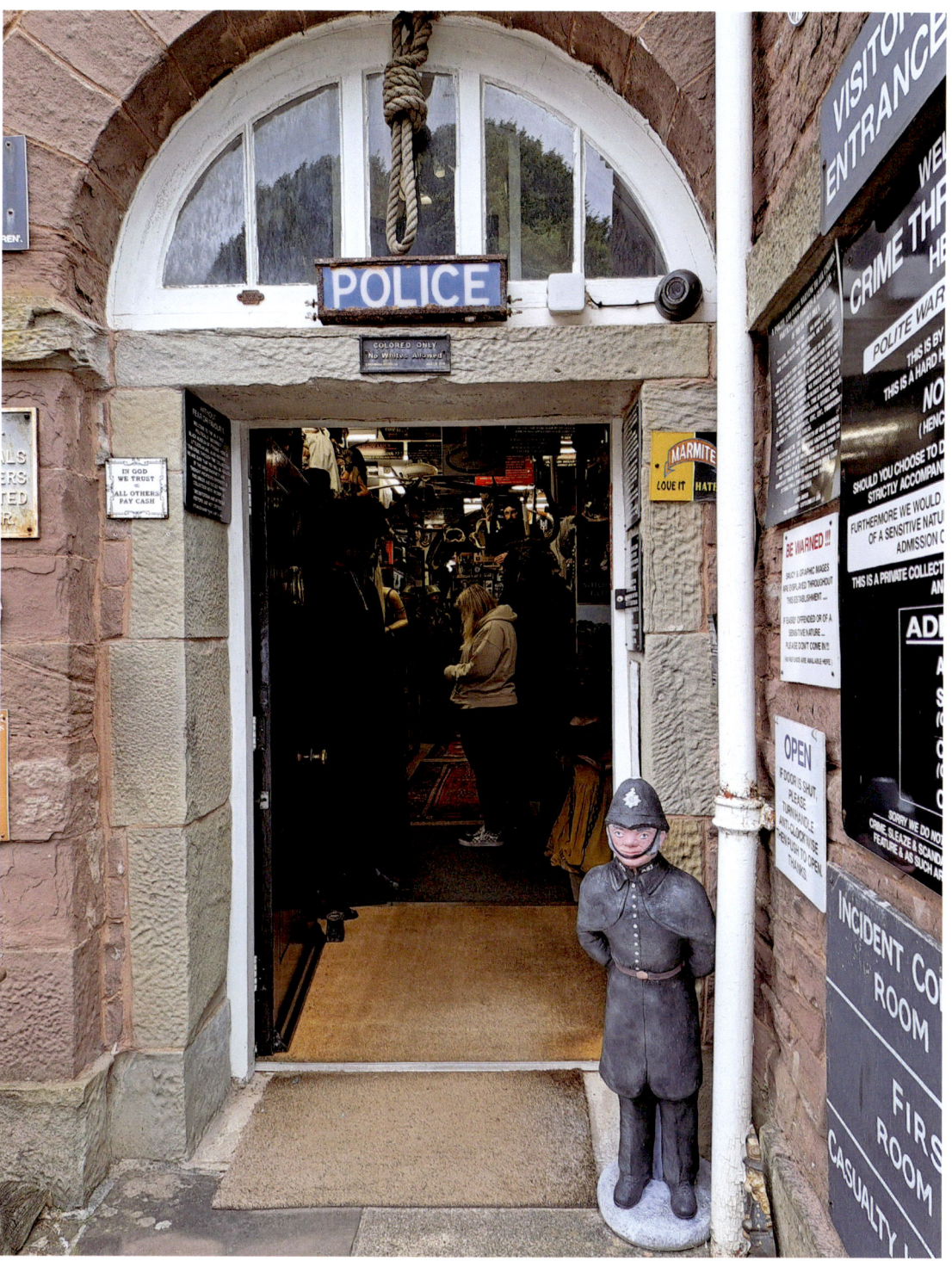

View into the interior of the museum, Littledean.

Littledean Hall

Known in the Guiness Book of records as 'the oldest inhabited house in England', Littledean Hall – or the site on which it stands – has persisted as a centre of human occupation and activity in various forms for over a thousand years. It has also been described as 'the most haunted house in Britain.' Some parapsychologists have theorised that 'an energy vortex appears to emanate' from the cellar under the north front, 'and may be the cause of the sensations and supernatural happenings in the house above'. A probable Saxon chapel has been discovered there, and Celtic remains uncovered on the site. Testing found the Celtic remains dated back to the 5th century. Re-used Roman masonry has also been found in the cellar along with Norman pottery.

The property has long been a location for unnerving experiences: 'a large damp grey-rendered building with gargoyles … full of hidden passageways and priest holes', according to Don Macer-Wright, author and archaeologist, whose family have lived in various parts of the Hall since 1955. Don says:

> It is the jackdaws … which in my mind most mark the indelible spirit of Littledean Hall. For more than a century, if not since their enemies, the ravens, disappeared, the jackdaws have roosted at the Hall in their hundreds … they now breed more in the ancient trees surrounding the place and, if anything, there are more of these birds than ever.

These birds and indeed all members of the corvid family have an undoubted mystique and that will be emphasised by a mysterious story I repeat later in my account of the Littledean Roman Temple excavations.

Don is the author of *The Hauntings of Littledean Hall*. He says

> The Hall, a structure of many phases built over the centuries since before the Norman Conquest, has locked within its very fabric imprinted emotions of both past and present, like an indelible photograph… the imprint is picked up by sensitive people… this would account for the reason why at Littledean Hall, so many different sorts of ghostly sightings and experiences have been witnessed.

Within the last 300 years of British history several tragic events have led to multiple reports of hauntings at Littledean Hall.

The first dates back to the period of the English Civil War, when a Royalist garrison was stationed at the Hall. During one incident in 1643, nearby Royalist soldiers had surrendered but someone in the house fired a pistol causing the Roundheads to attack. Colonel Congreve and Colonel Wigmore were both put to the sword in the dining room; it is reported that bloodstains continually re-emerge on the floorboards where they fell, even despite the boards being replaced. Also, shadowy cavaliers are seen in the courtyard.

Another story concerns the often-seen 'ghost of the black boy' who haunts the first-floor landing, candle in hand. An anonymous reporter from *The Fortean Times* saw him running across the landing then disappear. It is also believed this spectral visitant is responsible for poltergeist activity. A visitor in the 1950s slept extremely badly due to the lights flickering under the bedroom door, which the residents attributed to 'the black boy – he always haunted the landing'.

The boy's mischievous ghost is blamed for pulling flowers out of vases in the old dining room at night and throwing them into the fireplace, and for continually taking the same painting down from the wall and leaving it lying on the floor. The painting shows him with his young white master, Charles Pyrke, thought to have been the same age as him. An attempt was made to secure the painting by hanging it up with a strong chain, but it was discovered on the floor once more the next morning with the chain broken. The painting was subsequently removed, stored in a secret location, and replaced by a reproduction.

Charles was the son of Captain Thomas Pyrke, sugar plantation owner. The Pyrke family had purchased the property in 1664, and their descendants were to continue there for another 250 years. There are conflicting stories about the tragedy that took place in 1741; one version says Charles was accused of raping his servant's sister and fathering her new-born baby, who was 'concealed behind a secret panel in the Blue Bedroom'. That bedroom now is considered 'too haunted to sleep in'. The story relates how the young servant murdered Charles before escaping from the Hall;,but was later captured, brought back, and put to death. However, another version implies that Charles killed the young servant. Whatever happened, it has left intense ghostly activity imprinted within the fabric of the house.

The apparition of a monk is also reported to cross the dining room and enter the old library where a priest hole gave access to a tunnel below the cellar leading to the Grange of Flaxley Abbey a quarter of a mile away. The tunnel would have been used by monks to enter and exit the house to give Holy Communion without being seen, in the late sixteenth century.

Horses' hooves are heard in empty stables; some people suffer vertigo on the front staircase. Author Eddy Burke believes a previous occupant died falling down the stairs and is trapped here. Two other Pyrke brothers are said to wander the halls, having killed each other in a duel in 1740.

Remains of a Roman road have been found under the driveway and the ghostly top halves of a legion of Roman soldiers sighted along the old road. The fleeting image of a Roman has also been glimpsed at the outstanding ritual site not far away: a Roman temple in the outer part of the grounds. First discovered by Don Macer-Wright in 1984, it was identified by Professor Barri Jones in the same year as a second-to-third-century water shrine (a place dedicated to a nymph), which Dr Anne Ross considered may have been a cult shrine of Sabrina, the Welsh goddess (or nymph) of the River Severn. Sabrina is shown in Celtic myth as riding the Severn Bore in a chariot drawn by four horses. Recent excavations between 2018 and 2023 have produced much more evidence for a water shrine, which is reassessed, more specifically, as a Romano-British nymphaeum (a monument consecrated to the nymphs, especially those of springs). Don Macer-Wright describes an extraordinary phenomenon which took place there one autumn day in 1997.

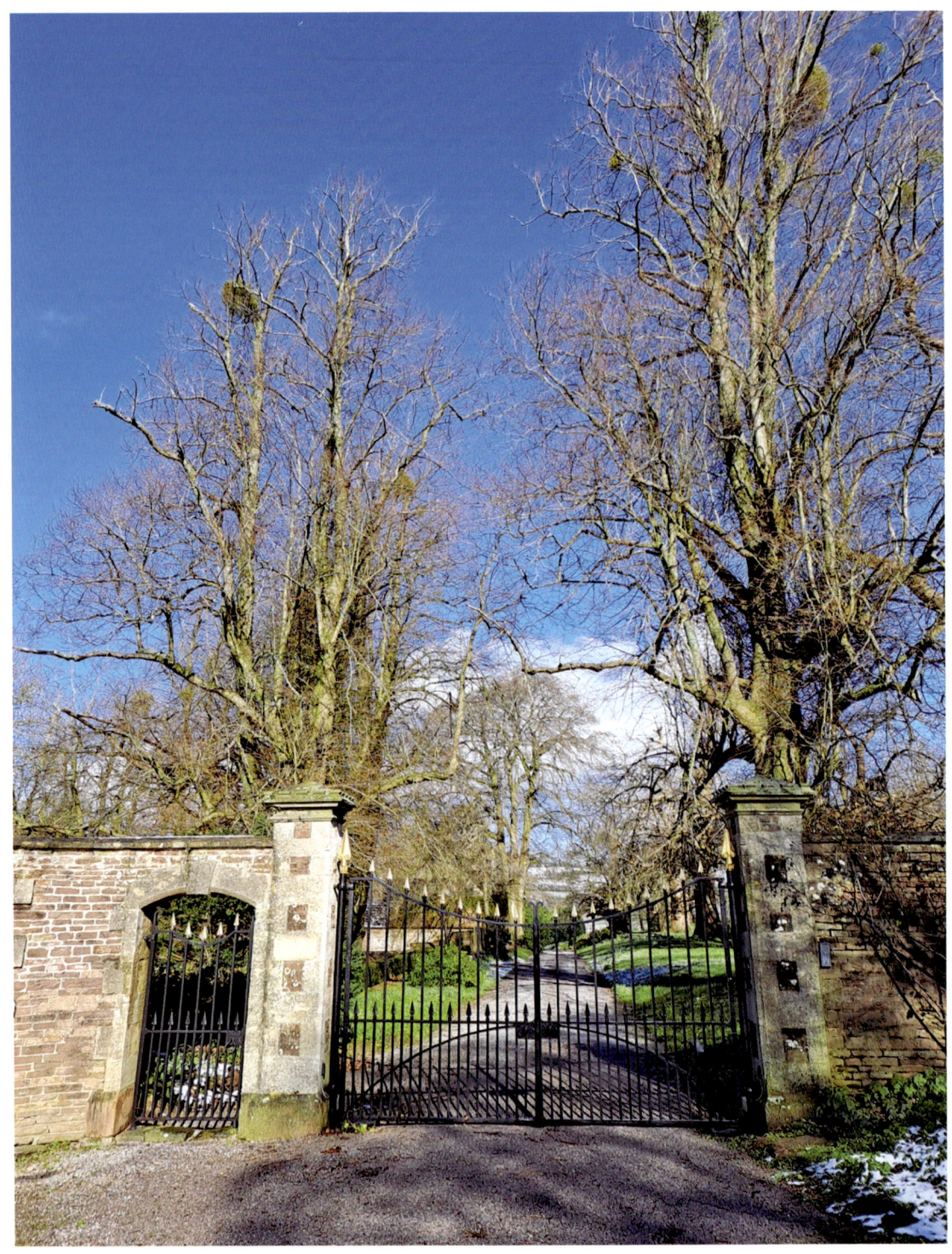

The drive to Littledean Hall is sited over a former Roman road.

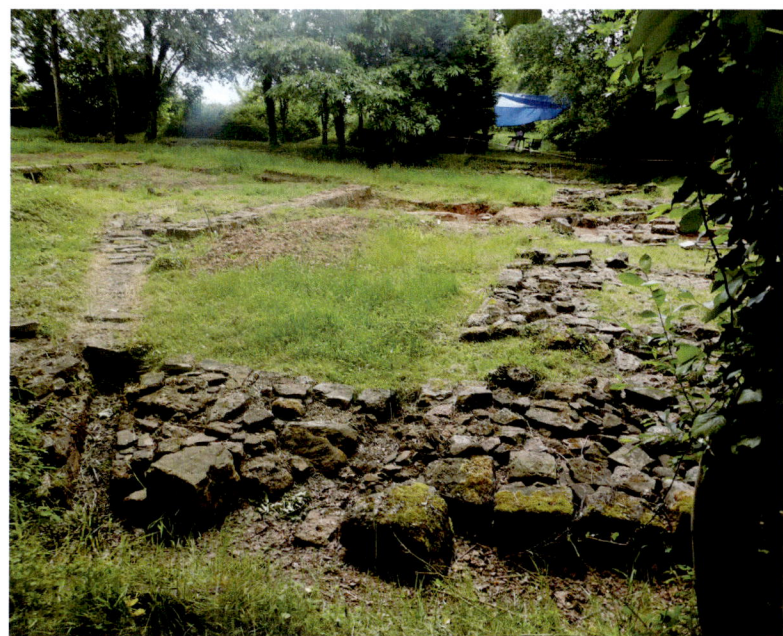

Roman temple excavations in the outer grounds at Littledean Hall. (Courtesy of Jamie Robinson)

> I had a visitor, a 'fey' with me. ('Fey' is a Celtic term meaning a person with supernatural abilities.) We were standing within the remains of the Roman temple. She suddenly asked me to be quiet and assumed a stance in which, pointing her forefinger somewhat aimlessly, she stood on one foot and with one eye closed … Within seconds the air was full of black birds; not just jackdaws but rooks, crows, ravens and even a number of blackbirds. They had all appeared as if by magic and the air was full of the most raucous and disturbed calls. There must have been several hundred birds all cavorting above our heads in what I can only describe as a chaotic dance of flight. In all my years as a countryman, I have never witnessed a more eerie and astonishing spectacle. The birds departed with a suddenness and speed, just as they had arrived, and the air and surroundings immediately returned to normality.

This site has a strong spiritual resonance, which I sensed during my visit. Originally the location was probably chosen because of the view of the Horseshoe Bend, which can be considered the largest and most significant topographical feature of its type in the Celtic World and was no doubt an inspiration to both the Ancient Celts and to the Romans. They would have observed the river, tides, and moon. They understood the moon rises, the moon sets, and at the full moon you have big tides on the river; these would all have added up to something very mystical at this location. Within the site, evidence has also been found of a Bronze Age cremation cemetery and Iron Age mortuary remains. Amongst the many artefacts discovered, incised stones with pictorial representations of heads are now being studied. Of particular interest are the 'ladder stones' with images of a ladder, a platform, and a rising or setting sun. It is thought these depicted the stairway to the heavens, being symbolic images associated with death and found all round the world. These stones found at the Littledean Roman Temple site are most likely at least 4,000 years old.

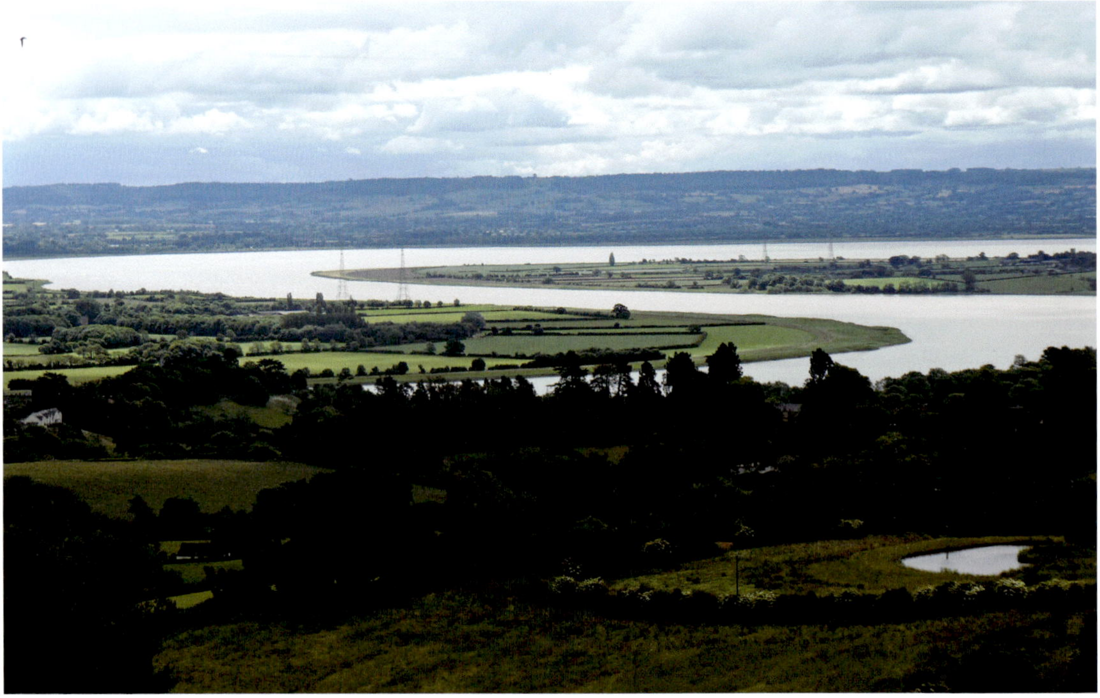

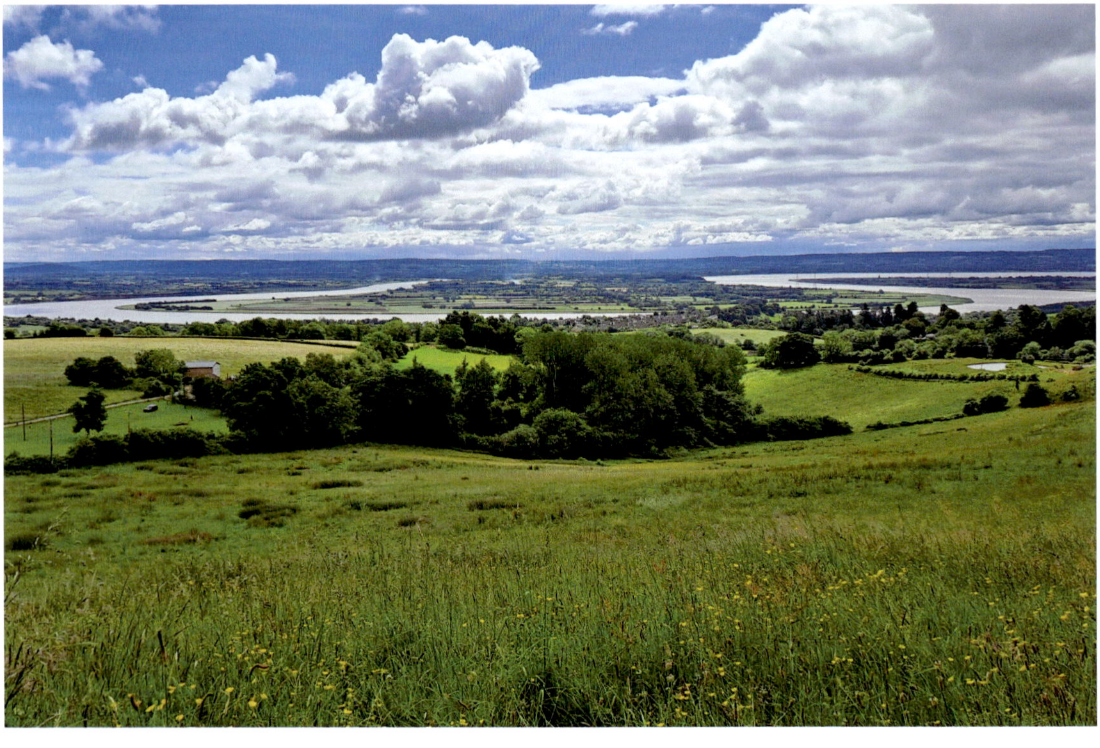

The Horseshoe Bend of the River Severn. (Courtesy of Jamie Robinson)

13

Chipping Sodbury

The actors are at hand and by their show
You shall know all that you are like to know.
A Midsummer Night's Dream, Act 5, Scene 1

Horton Court

The Tudor Gothic property known as Horton Court, built in 1520, is located on Horton Road next to the Church of St James the Elder near Chipping Sodbury. This church itself dates back to 1300 and stands on the site of earlier Anglo Saxon and then Norman places of worship. In Norman times the vicar lived in the Vicar's Hall, now part of Horton Court, thought to be one of the oldest clergy residences remaining in the country; parts of that building date back to 1160.

The quiet and almost dreamlike location is reached by steep, narrow, winding lanes through dense woodlands, scattered with millions of wild garlic flowers in the springtime. In fact one visitor described the approach lanes to the property as 'not for the faint-hearted'. The house and grounds, however, seemed a perfect film location for a story of the supernatural called *The Living and the Dead*. Like Chavenage, Horton Court is popular among filmmakers and has been used as a set for *Wolf Hall* and *Poldark*; and, also like Chavenage, it is not short on eerie happenings.

Filming of *The Living and the Dead* took place in 2016 starring Colin Morgan and Charlotte Spencer. When journalist Huw Fullerton interviewed the actors for a *Radio Times* article, he got more than he bargained for, along with his fellow journalists. The interview venue was the disused 'secret Catholic chapel', formed by the addition of a floor to the Norman hall in 1708. Several journalists sat here with the actors, writer and producer, who all had plenty to say about the unsettling events that took place during their film shoot.

Actress Charlotte Spencer described how on one occasion they were filming, and she heard footsteps: 'I turned around thinking they would run away... the first assistant director was about to say, "Who's walking in the corridor?" and there was no one there. They were the loudest footsteps I've ever heard down the corridor, and Sound never picked it up.'

Her co-star Colin Morgan noted that the history of the set had some uncanny similarities to the plot of their drama: 'Supposedly a boy did drown in the lake in the 1930s ... a similar drowning takes place in the series, which mainly focuses on my character and his wife returning to the family farm only to encounter a series of supernatural occurrences that test their marriage. I hope it's coincidence.'

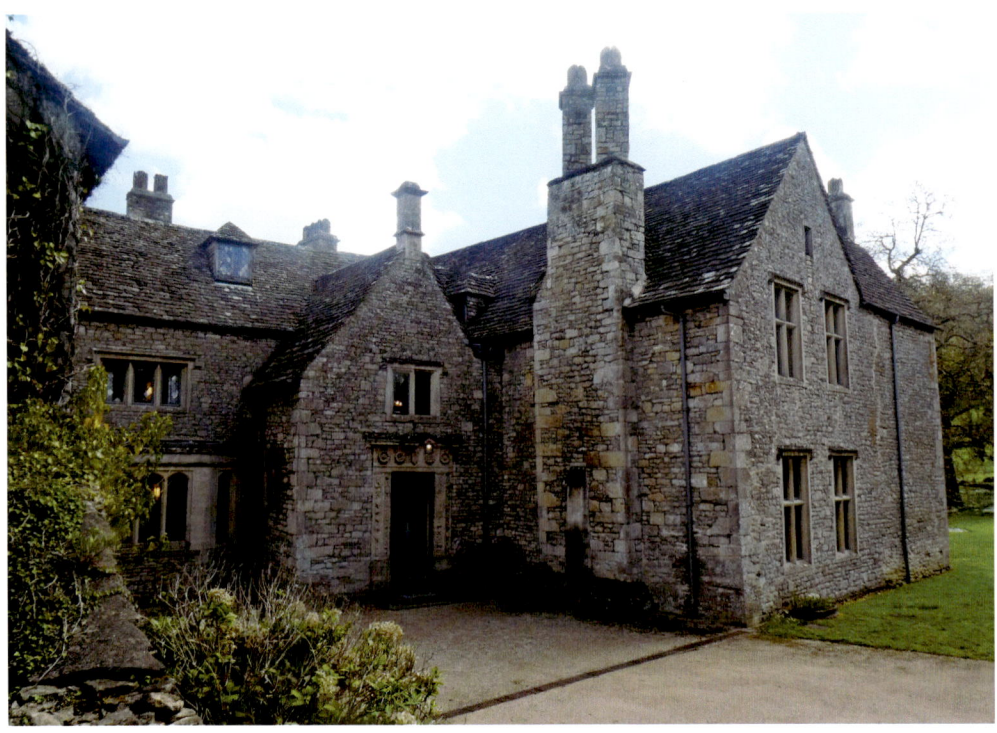

Horton Court, viewed from the churchyard. (Courtesy of Jamie Robinson)

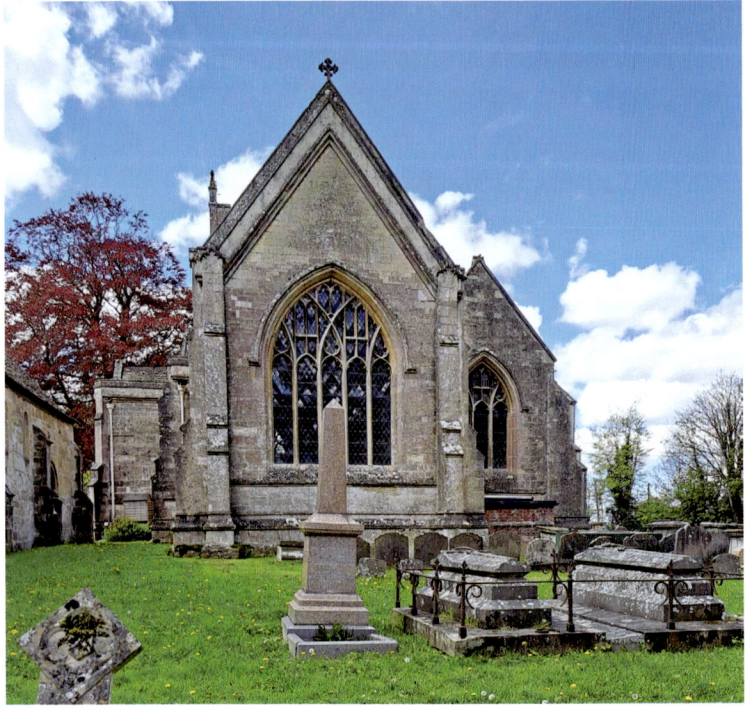

The Church of
St James the Elder at
Horton Court.

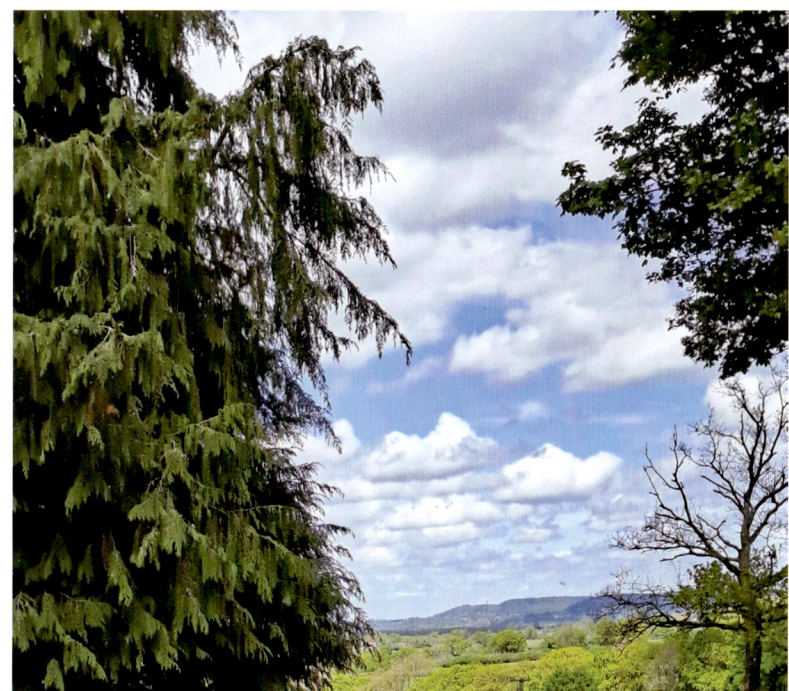

Countryside
surrounding
Horton Court.

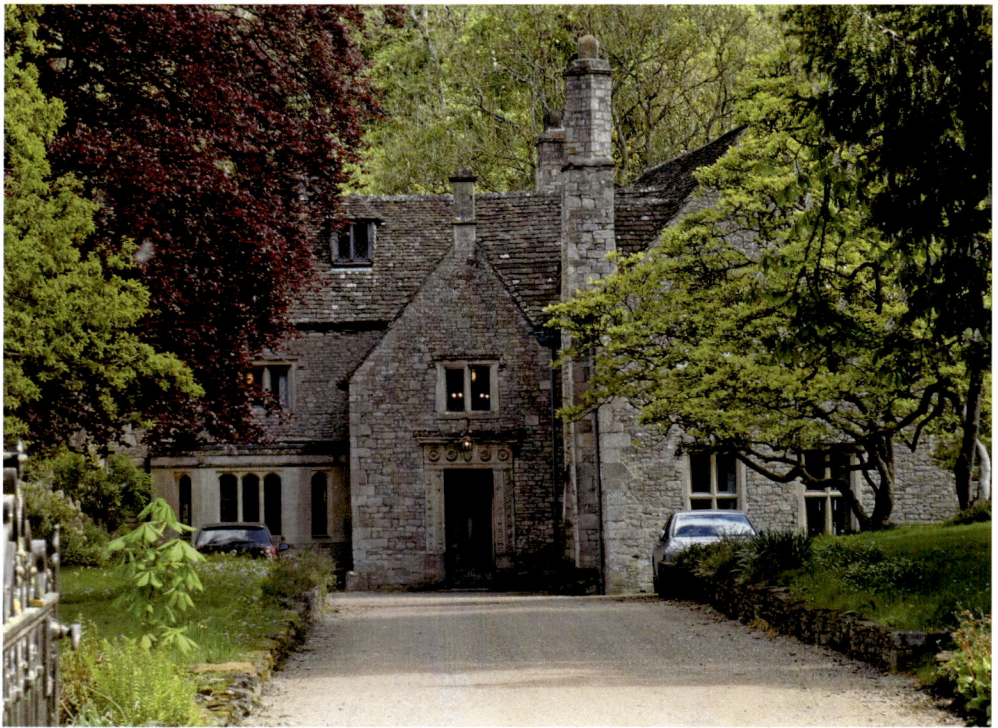

Horton Court. (Courtesy of Jamie Robinson)

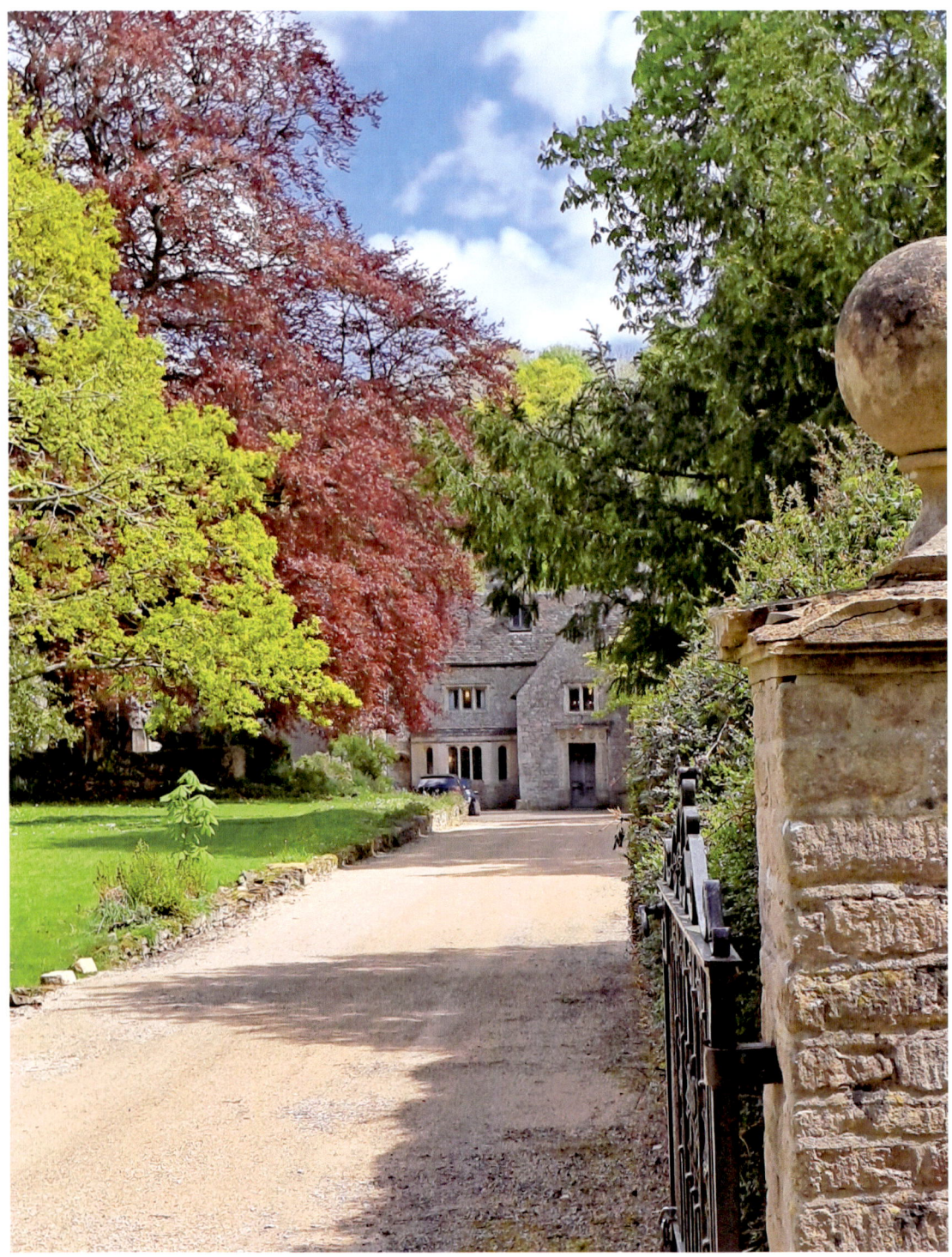

Horton Court as seen from the entrance gateway.

The journalists valiantly strove to make light of the stories they heard from actors and crew, but the longer they listened, the less sceptical they became.

One anecdote originated with a child of the family who occupied Horton Court during the 1930s. He regularly saw the apparition of an old lady who would appear at night and stand over his bed. The household was unaware of this until the boy shared the details with them.

Fast-forward to 2016 and the increasingly unnerved journalists discovered that actors and crew had also noted 'the shadowy figure lurking at the back of scenes who was later nowhere to be found; the mysterious footsteps ringing down the corridors while they did a second take; the filming of a séance interrupted by an angry flurry of flying papers, a moment actually caught on camera'.

Producer Eliza Mellor had two distinctly uncanny recollections:

> We were filming a sequence with Colin who was doing the Ouija board scene where he's calling up the ghosts. He was calling out, 'Are you there? Are you there?' and suddenly all these papers flew off the shelf onto the floor and we were all really freaked out … The next moment we were filming again, and somebody said, 'Oh, there's somebody in there, can you move out of the way,' and then we went in and there was nobody there. We all looked and played back, and it really looked like somebody had been there.

The interviewer noted that 'the heating breaks in the disused chapel we're using for interviews, and a chill runs through us all. I pull on gloves and check the time on my phone to see how much longer we have to stay here'.

Most striking of all was the strange incident with the telephone; the journalists were spooked by this one when they discovered that their mobile phone batteries had lost charge. Co-creator and writer Ashley Pharoah says that while they were filming they heard a telephone ring. 'We were saying "God, that's really odd, like old fashioned telephone rings. Why is the phone ringing?" We went down to talk to the National Trust, and they said the phones had been cut off for years.'

At this point, the journalist checked his own mobile phone and saw that despite being on seventy per-cent charge ten minutes before, it had gone dark 'stone dead'. Near the end of the day he checked with his colleagues; two more phones had blacked out and others had lost signal.

Charlotte Spencer sums up with these words about Horton Court: 'I don't get a bad feeling in this house. I wouldn't dismiss it or say, "Yes there definitely is something," but I don't get a bad feeling. It's more that they're interested. I wouldn't spend a night in there by myself. There would have to be a big group of people.'

Ashley Pharoah remarks: 'We all like being a little frightened from time to time. I think everyone's on the same journey as an ending. Everybody is interested in what the next great adventure is, and I think people like to be scared.'

He concludes, 'it's a really ancient need to sit around a fire and tell ghost stories.' William Shakespeare would, I believe, agree with him. As he says, through the mouth of *Richard II*, Act III, Scene 2:

> For God's sake, let us sit upon the ground
> And tell sad stories of the death of kings;
> How some have been deposed; some slain in war,
> Some haunted by the ghosts they have deposed…

Bibliography

Jarvis, Katie, 'Triumph Over Trials, the story of Elizabeth, Lady Ashcombe, at Sudeley Castle', *Cotswold Life Magazine*, Summer (2024), pp. 14–19

Hartsiotis, Kirsty, 'Walk: Ghostly Tale and a Bloody Meadow', *Cotswold Life Magazine* (October 2023), pp. 142–144

Andrews, Ross, *Paranormal Cheltenham* (Amberley Publishing, 2009)

Linnell, B. R., *Tewkesbury Pubs* (Theoc Press, 1996)

Howard, Jonathan, *A Thousand Fancies: The Collection of Charles Wade of Snowshill Manor* (Pitkin Publishing, 2016)

Cass, Matt, and James, Paul, *100 Facts, Myths & Legends About the Cotswolds* (2023)

Holland, Richard, *The Cotwolds Ghost Stories* (Bradwell Books, 2014)

Tewkesbury Abbey, *Tewkesbury Abbey* (Scala Arts & Heritage Publishers, 2012)

Berkeley Castle, *Berkeley Castle* (Scala Arts & Heritage Publishers, 2013)

Hart-Davis, Duff, *Woodchester Mansion Guide Book* (Woodchester Mansion Trust Ltd., 5th edition)

Fullard, John (ed.) and Lister, Margaret (photographer), *Woodchester Mansion, Artistry's haunting curse – the incomplete* (Benwell Publishing, 2014)

Howley, Chris, *The Ghosts of Woodchester Mansion* (Woodchester Mansion Trust, 2016)

Davenport, Liz, *Why Was Woodchester Mansion Never Finished? Plans Post 1873* (Woodchester Mansion Trust, 2016)

Davenport, Liz, *William Leigh: Success or Failure?* (Woodchester Mansion Trust, 2016)

Mander, Nicholas, *Owlpen Manor: A Short History and Guide* (The Owlpen Press, 2006)

Comstock, Francis, *A Gothic Vision: F. L. Griggs and His Work* (Ashmolean Museum, 1966)

Macer-Wright, Donald, *The Hauntings of Littledean Hall* (Douglas McLean, 2011)

Online Sources

Mysteriouspeople.com

'The Haunted West Country Journals', Facebook, 30 July 2022

weird-world.net/haunted-Gloucester

bbc.co.uk/history

soglos.com/visit/the-most-haunted-places-in-Gloucestershire

Online article by Lisa Capener on visitcheltenham.com: 'Ghostly Goings on in
 Cheltenham'
'Montpellier and Pittville, Cheltenham', cotswoldplaces.com/haunted-places
'The Morton Case, Cheltenham' soglos.com/Gloucestershire-literary-legends
'Belas Knap Long Barrow', article by Andy Lloyd and Martin Cosnette, posted online
 13 April 2005
Darren Baldwin's story of his Prestbury experience, bbc.co.uk
'The most haunted place in England?', gloucestershirepubs.co.uk/bell-hotel-tewkesbury
'Michele Eve', mysticaltimesblog.com
'The Hauntings of Arlingham Gloucestershire', mysticaltimesblog.com hauntedrooms.
 co.uk
'Gloucestershire Spookiest', gloucestershirelive.co.uk
'Most Haunted Places in Cirencester Revealed', wiltsglosstandard.co.uk
owlpen.com
The story of Thomas Daunt the Seventh
hauntedhovel.com
'Owlpen Manor', hauntedplaces.org
yourparanormal.com (accessed 6 November 2023)
'Cotswolds Ghost Story', brian-haughton.com

Acknowledgements

Every attempt has been made to seek permission for copyright material used in this book. However, if we have inadvertently used copyright material without permission or acknowledgement, we apologise and we will make the necessary correction at the first opportunity. The author would like to thank the following people and companies for assistance with historical accuracy, and permission to use stories, quotes and photographs:

Liz Davenport, Archivist, Woodchester Mansion Trust.

Caroline and George Lowsley-Williams, Chavenage House (to arrange a visit, contact Historic Houses).

Radio Times for permission to quote from an interview carried out by Huw Fullerton and published online on 17 June 2016: radiotimes.com/tv/drama/my day on the haunted set of the living and the dead.

Caroline Humphries, the Ancient Ram Inn. For event bookings, see ancientraminn. co.uk.

The author would like to thank the members of the Mander family for their willingness to share both historical and paranormal tales during a fascinating tour of Owlpen Manor (to arrange a visit, contact Historic Houses).